P9-DMT-061

Critical acclaim for Primo Levi

"Primo Levi is that rare individual, a survivor who can write of his experiences, yet keep a sense of balance and proportion. . . . His works prove that a perceptive observer and a skilled writer can indeed penetrate the deepest feelings of horror."

—*San Francisco Chronicle*

"One of the most important and gifted writers of our time"

—Italo Calvino

"Primo Levi creates for us a miniature universe of moral striving and reflectiveness, filtered through ordeals of memory reinforced by resources of imagination. When I read his books I feel an exhilarating closeness."

—Irving Howe

"Primo Levi is a memoirist with a difference."

—*Newsday*

"I consider Primo Levi one of the most important Italian writers and I am proud that I was on the jury that awarded him the coveted Viareggio Prize."

—Umberto Eco

"Primo Levi's books are a study of the limits of being human. His subject is everyday life at Auschwitz. His forte is the anecdote, the character sketch, the singular fact that quickens an experience we would rather forget or confronts us with a conundrum we would rather ignore. . . . Levi makes no excuses, he offers no interpretations. He describes. And ultimately the reviewer is left with only one thing to say: READ."

—*Washington Post Book World*

PENGUIN BOOKS

MOMENTS OF REPRIEVE

Primo Levi was born in Turin, Italy, in 1919 and was trained as a chemist. Arrested as a member of the antifascist resistance, he was deported to Auschwitz in 1944 and spent ten months there before the arrival of the Red Army. Levi's experience in the death camp and his subsequent travels through Eastern Europe are the subject of his two classic memoirs, *Survival in Auschwitz* and *The Reawakening*. He is also the author of *The Periodic Table* and *If Not Now, When?* (Penguin), which won the distinguished Viareggio and Campiello prizes when published in Italy in 1982. Dr. Levi retired from his position as manager of a Turin chemical factory in 1977 in order to devote himself full time to writing. He died in 1987.

Ruth Feldman has received the John Florio and Circe-Sabaudia prizes for her Italian translations. She lives in Cambridge, Massachusetts.

MOMENTS OF REPRIEVE

PRIMO LEVI

TRANSLATED FROM THE ITALIAN
BY RUTH FELDMAN

PENGUIN BOOKS

PENGUIN BOOKS
Published by the Penguin Group
Viking Penguin, a division of Penguin Books USA Inc.,
375 Hudson Street, New York, New York 10014, U.S.A.
Penguin Books Ltd, 27 Wrights Lane, London W8 5TZ, England
Penguin Books Australia Ltd, Ringwood, Victoria, Australia
Penguin Books Canada Ltd, 10 Alcorn Avenue, Suite 300,
Toronto, Ontario, Canada M4V 3B2
Penguin Books (N.Z.) Ltd, 182–190 Wairau Road,
Auckland 10, New Zealand

Penguin Books Ltd, Registered Offices:
Harmondsworth, Middlesex, England

First published in the United States of America by
Summit Books, A Division of Simon & Schuster, Inc., 1986
Published in Penguin Books 1987

10   9   8   7   6   5

Translation copyright © Summit Books, A Division of
Simon & Schuster, Inc., 1979, 1981, 1982, 1983, 1986
Copyright © Giulio Einaudi editore s.p.a., 1981, 1985
All rights reserved

Some of the translations of the stories have been
previously published in periodical form. Most
of the stories have been previously published in
Italian in *Lilit e altri racconti*.

LIBRARY OF CONGRESS CATALOGING IN PUBLICATION DATA
Levi, Primo.
Moments of reprieve.
   "Most of the stories have been previously published
in Italian in Lilit e altri racconti."—
   1. Levi, Primo—Biography—Imprisonment—Poland—
Oświęcim. 2. World War, 1939–1945—Personal narratives,
Italian. 3. World War, 1939–1945—Prisoners and
prisons, German. 4. Auschwitz (Poland : Concentration
camp). 5. Authors, Italian—20th century—Biography.
   6. Prisoners of war—Italy—Biography. 7. Prisoners
of war—Poland—Biography. I. Title.
PQ4872.E8Z4713   1987   853'.914   [B]   86-16858
ISBN 0 14 00.9370 2

Printed in the United States of America
Set in Electra

Except in the United States of America,
this book is sold subject to the condition
that it shall not, by way of trade or otherwise,
be lent, re-sold, hired out, or otherwise circulated
without the publisher's prior consent in any form of
binding or cover other than that in which it is
published and without a similar condition
including this condition being imposed
on the subsequent purchaser

Contents

Preface

Writing and publishing *Survival in Auschwitz* (1947) and *The Reawakening* (1963) marked a decisive turn in my life, and not only my life as a writer. For several years afterward, I had the feeling that I had performed a task, indeed the only task clearly defined for me. At Auschwitz, and on the long road returning home, I had seen and experienced things that appeared important not only for me, things that imperiously demanded to be told. And I had told them, I had testified. I was a chemist, I had a profession which gave me a living and wholly absorbed me, I did not feel the need to write anything else.

But things have not gone that way. With the passing of the years, writing has made a space for itself alongside my professional activity and I have ended up by switching to it entirely. At the same time I realized that my experience of Auschwitz was far from exhausted. I had described its fundamental features, which today have a historical pertinence, in my first two books, but a host of details continued to surface in my memory and the idea of letting them fade

9

10   away distressed me. A great number of human figures especially stood out against that tragic background: friends, people I'd traveled with, even adversaries—begging me one after
another to help them survive and enjoy the ambiguous peren-
nial existence of literary characters. This was no longer the
anonymous, faceless, voiceless mass of the shipwrecked, but
the few, the different, the ones in whom (if only for a moment) I had recognized the will and capacity to react, and
hence a rudiment of virtue.

In these stories, written at different times and on different occasions, and certainly not planned, a common trait
seems to appear: each of them is centered on one character
only, who never is the persecuted, predestined victim, the
prostrate man, the person to whom I had devoted my first
book, and about whom I had obsessively asked myself if this
was still a man. The protagonists of these stories are "men"
beyond all doubt, even if the virtue that allows them to survive and makes them unique is not always one approved of
by common morality. Bandi, my "disciple," draws strength
from the blessed gaiety of believers, Wolf from music, Grigo
from love and superstition, Tischler from the patrimony of
legends; but Cesare draws his from unbridled cunning, Rumkowski from the thirst for power, Rappoport from a feral
vitality.

Rereading the stories I notice another peculiarity: the
scenarios that I selected spontaneously are hardly ever tragic.
They are bizarre, marginal moments of reprieve, in which the
compressed identity can reacquire for a moment its linea-
ments.

The reader may be surprised at this rediscovered narra-
tive vein, thirty or forty years after the events. Well, it has
been observed by psychologists that the survivors of traumatic events are divided into two well-defined groups: those
who repress their past *en bloc*, and those whose memory
of the offense persists, as though carved in stone, prevailing

over all previous or subsequent experiences. Now, not by choice but by nature, I belong to the second group. Of my two years of life outside the law I have not forgotten a single thing. Without any deliberate effort, memory continues to restore to me events, faces, words, sensations, as if at that time my mind had gone through a period of exalted receptivity, during which not a detail was lost. I remember, for example, as they would be remembered by a tape recorder or a parrot, whole sentences in languages I did not know then, and don't know now. A few years ago I met, after thirty-five years, a fellow prisoner with whom I had not had any special friendship, and I recognized him immediately in the midst of a great number of unknown faces, although his physiognomy was greatly changed. Smells from "down there" startle me even now. It seems to me obvious today that this attention of mine at that time, turned to the world and to the human beings around me, was not only a symptom but also an important factor of spiritual and physical salvation.

It is possible that the distance in time has accentuated the tendency to round out the facts or heighten the colors: this tendency, or temptation, is an integral part of writing, without it one does not write stories but rather accounts. Nevertheless, the episodes on which I have built each of these stories actually did take place, and the characters did exist, even if, for obvious reasons, I have often changed their names.

PRIMO LEVI

THE SURVIVOR

to B. V.

Dopo di allora, ad ora incerta,

Since then, at an uncertain hour,
That agony returns:
And till my ghastly tale is told,
This heart within me burns.

Once again he sees his companions' faces
Livid in the first faint light,
Gray with cement dust,
Nebulous in the mist,
Tinged with death in their uneasy sleep.
At night, under the heavy burden
Of their dreams, their jaws move,
Chewing a nonexistent turnip.
"Stand back, leave me alone, submerged people,
Go away. I haven't dispossessed anyone,
Haven't usurped anyone's bread.
No one died in my place. No one.
Go back into your mist.
It's not my fault if I live and breathe,
Eat, drink, sleep and put on clothes."

Rappoport's Testament

I T WAS IMPOSSIBLE to love or hate Valerio. His limitations, his deficiencies relegated him, from the very first, to a place outside the usual relationships between men. He had been short and fat; he was still short, and the flaccid folds on his face and body testified sadly to his former corpulence. We had worked together for a long time in the Polish mud. All of us had fallen in the deep slippery workyard mud but, thanks to that bit of animal nobility that survives even in a man reduced to despair, we struggled to avoid falling, and to minimize its effects; in fact, a man prostrate on the ground is endangered, for he stirs fierce instincts, and inspires derision rather than pity. Unlike the rest of us, Valerio fell continually, more than anyone else. It took only the slightest bump, and not even that. It was obvious that at times he let himself fall on purpose, if someone just insulted him or moved to strike him. Down he went from his low height into the

18   mud, as if it were his mother's breast, as though the erect
position were in itself temporary, as it is for someone who
walks on stilts. The mud was his refuge, his apparent defense. He was a little mud man, and the color of mud
was his color. He knew it, and with the modicum of intelligence which suffering had left him he knew he was a
laughingstock.

And he talked about it, because he talked a lot. End-
lessly he recounted his misadventures, the falls, slaps,
mockery, like a sad Punch who did not try to spare a
particle of himself or leave the most abject details veiled.
He even dramatized the more awkward aspects of his
misfortunes with a touch of theatrical flamboyance, in
which remnants of convivial good nature could be detected. Anyone who knows men like him knows that they
are flatterers by nature and without ulterior motives. If
we had met in normal life I don't know what he would
have found to flatter me about; there in the Camp, every
morning he complimented me on my healthy look. Although I wasn't all that superior to him, I felt pity for
him, along with a slight feeling of irritation. But pity in
those days, since one couldn't act on it, was dispelled almost on conception, like smoke in the wind, leaving an
empty taste of hunger in the mouth. Like all the others,
I tried more or less consciously to avoid him: his degree
of need was too evident, and in someone in need one always sees a creditor.

One gloomy September day the air-raid sirens
sounded across the mud, rising and falling in tone like a

long feral moan. This was nothing new, and I had a secret hiding place: a subterranean bowel where bales of empty sacks were piled up. I went down, and there I found Valerio. He greeted me with wordy cordiality (barely reciprocated), and without delay, as I was starting to fall asleep, began telling me his bad-luck stories. Outside, after the sirens' tragic howl, a threatening silence reigned, but all at once we heard a heavy tread and immediately afterwards saw the huge black outline of Rappoport at the top of the stairs, with a pail in his hand. He saw us, cried "Italians!" and let go of the pail, which rolled with a clatter down the steps.

The pail had contained soup, but it was now empty, almost clean. Valerio and I got some leftover bits, carefully scraping the bottom and sides with the spoons which, in those days, we kept with us day and night, ready for any and every improbable emergency, the way the Knights Templar bore their swords. In the meantime, Rappoport had descended majestically among us: he was not a man to give away soup or ask for it.

At that time Rappoport could have been about thirty-five. A Pole by origin, he had taken his degree in medicine in Pisa. Hence his liking for Italians, and his lopsided friendship with Valerio, who had been born in Pisa. Rappoport was admirably armed. Shrewd, violent, and happy as the adventurers of earlier days, it had been easy for him to leave behind, at one fell swoop, whatever civilian education he found superfluous. He lived in the Camp like a tiger in the jungle, striking down and practicing extortion on the weak, and avoiding those who

20   were stronger; ready to corrupt, steal, fight, pull in his belt, lie, or play up to you, depending on the circumstances. He was therefore an enemy, but not despicable or repugnant. He slowly descended the stairs, and when he got close, we could clearly see where the contents of the pail had ended up. This was one of his specialties: at the first wail of the air-raid alarm, in the general turmoil he would dash to the workyard kitchen and escape with his booty before the patrol arrived. He had gotten away with this three times; the fourth time, like the prudent bandit that he was, he remained quietly with his squad during the entire alarm. Lilienthal, who tried to imitate him, was caught in the act and publicly hanged the next day.

"Greetings, Italians," he said. "*Ciao, pisano!*" Then there was silence. We stretched out on the sacks, side by side, and soon Valerio and I slipped into a doze that teemed with images. A horizontal position was not a requisite: in moments of rest we fell asleep on our feet. But not Rappoport, who, even though he detested work, had one of those sanguine temperaments that cannot bear inaction. He took a small knife out of his pocket and began to sharpen it on a stone, spitting on the blade at intervals. But even that was not enough for him. He addressed Valerio, who was already snoring.

"Wake up, boy; what were you dreaming about? Ravioli, right? and Chianti wine, at the student mess in Via dei Mille, for a few lire. And the steaks, *psza crew!* Black-market steaks that covered the whole plate. A great country, Italy. And then Margherita . . ." and here he grimaced genially, and beat a hand resoundingly on his thigh. Valerio had waked up and was squatting there with a smile curdled on his small ashen face. Very few people ever addressed a word to him but I don't think in his position it concerned him very much.

Rappoport, however, often spoke to him, letting himself go with sincere abandon on the wave of his Pisan memories. It was clear to me that for Rappoport, Valerio represented only a pretext for these moments of mental vacation. But for Valerio they were pledges of friendship, the precious friendship of someone with power, bestowed with a generous hand on him, man to man, if not exactly equal to equal.

"Come on: you mean to say you didn't know Margherita? Didn't you ever sleep with her? What kind of *pisano* are you? That was a woman to wake the dead; nice and neat in the daytime, and a real artist at night . . ." At this point we heard a whistle start up, and then, suddenly, another one. They seemed to have begun in some remote distance, but they were bearing down on us like locomotives in a mad race. The ground shook, the cement ceiling-beams vibrated for an instant as though they were made of rubber, and finally the two explosions matured, followed by a ruinous crash and the voluptuous relaxation in us of the spasm. Valerio had dragged himself into a corner, hidden his face in the crook of his elbow as if to protect himself from a slap, and was praying under his breath.

Another monstrous whistle sounded. The new European generations are not familiar with these whistles.

22   They could not have come about by chance: someone
must have wanted to endow the bombs with a voice that
expressed their thirst and their menace. I rolled down off
the sacks against the wall. Here it was, the explosion, very
close by, almost solid, like a body, and then the vast sigh
of the after-eddy. Rappoport cracked his jaws laughing.
"You filled your pants, eh, *pisano?* Or not yet? Well, just
wait, wait: the best is yet to come."

"You have good nerves," I said, while from my *liceo*
memories surfaced a vision—faded, as from a previous
incarnation—of the defiant image of Capaneus, challeng-
ing Jove from the depths of Hell and laughing at his
thunderbolts.

"It's not a matter of nerves but of theory. Of accounting. It's my secret weapon."

Now at that time I was bone-weary, with a by now
ancient, incarnate weariness that I thought irrevocable.
It was not the weariness known to most people, that
superimposes itself upon well-being and veils it like a
temporary paralysis, but rather it was a definitive void,
an amputation. I felt emptied, like a rifle that has been
fired. Valerio felt as I did, perhaps somewhat less consciously, and so did all the others. Rappoport's vitality,
which I would have admired under other circumstances
(and in fact admire today), appeared out of place and
insolent. If our skins weren't worth two cents, his skin,
for all that he was a Pole with a full belly, was not worth
much more, and it was irritating that he refused to recognize this. As for the business of theory and accounts, I
had no desire to hear about them. I had other things to

do, like sleeping, if the masters of the heavens permitted
it. If not, I wanted to savor my fear in peace, like any
proper person.

But it was not easy to repress, elude, or ignore Rappoport. "What are you sleeping for? Here I am about to
make my will and you're sleeping! Perhaps my bomb is
already on its way, and I don't want to miss this chance.
If I were free, I'd like to write a book with my philosophy
in it. But for now, all I can do is tell it to you two
wretches. If you can use it, fine. If not, and you get out
of here alive and I don't, which would be rather strange,
you can spread it about and maybe it will be of use to
somebody. Who knows? Not that it matters much to
me, though. I don't have the makings of a philanthropist.

"Well, here it is. While I could I drank, I ate, I
made love, I left flat gray Poland for that Italy of yours;
I studied, learned, traveled and looked at things. I kept
my eyes wide open; I didn't waste a crumb. I've been
diligent; I don't think I could have done more or better.
Things went well for me; I accumulated a large quantity
of good things, and all that good has not disappeared.
It's inside me, safe and sound. I don't let it fade; I've
held on to it. Nobody can take it from me.

"Then I wound up here. I've been in this place for
twenty months, and for twenty months I've been keeping
accounts. They balance—in fact I still have a substantial
credit. To tip the balance, it would take many more
months of Camp, or many days of torture. Actually"
(he caressed his stomach affectionately), "with a little
initiative, even here you can find something good every

24   so often. So in the sad event that one of you should survive me, you will be able to say that Leon Rappoport got
what was due him, left behind neither debits nor credits,
and did not weep or ask for pity. If I meet Hitler in the
other world, I'll spit in his face and I'll have every right
to . . ." A bomb fell nearby, followed by a roar like a
landslide. One of the warehouses must have collapsed.
Rappoport had to raise his voice almost to a shout: "because he didn't get the better of me."

I saw Rappoport again only once, for a few instants,
and his image has stayed with me in the almost photo-
graphic form of that last apparition. I was sick and in the
camp infirmary, in January 1945. From my bunk you
could see a stretch of street between two barracks where
a path had been worn in the snow, which was quite high
by now. The infirmary attendants often passed in pairs,
bearing dead or dying men on stretchers. One day I saw
two stretcher-bearers and one of them struck me because
of his tall stature and an imperious, authoritative obesity,
unusual in those places. I recognized Rappoport, got
down, went to the window, and rapped on the glass. He
stopped, directed a gay, meaningful grimace at me, and
raised his hand in an expansive greeting which made his
sad burden slide disjointedly to one side.

Two days later the Camp was evacuated, under
frightful circumstances which are now common knowledge. I have reason to believe that Rappoport did not
survive. So I considered it my duty to perform as best I
could the task with which I was entrusted.

The Juggler

WE CALLED THEM *"Grüne Spitzen"* (green triangles), common criminals, *Befauer*, from the initials BV with which they were officially designated, and which in turn was the abbreviation of something like "prisoners in preventive detention." We lived with them, obeyed, feared, and detested them, but knew almost nothing about them. For that matter, little is known even now. They were the "green triangles," Germans already held in regular prisons, who had been offered—according to mysterious criteria—the alternative of serving out their sentences in a Camp rather than a prison. As a rule they were scum. A lot of them boasted that they lived better in the Camp than at home, because, in addition to the heady pleasure of command, they were given a free hand with the rations allotted to us. Many were murderers in the narrow sense of the word. They made no secret of it and their behavior showed it.

28   Eddy (probably a stage name) was a green triangle but no murderer. He had two professions: he was a juggler and, in his spare time, a thief. In June of 1944 he became the vice Kapo of our squad, and he quickly struck us because of his uncommon qualities. Dazzlingly handsome, he was blond, of medium height, but slim, strong, and very agile. He had aristocratic features and skin so light it looked translucent. He could not have been more than twenty-three, and he didn't give a damn about anything or anyone: the SS, work, or us. He had a serene and self-absorbed look that set him apart. The very day of his arrival, he became famous. In the washroom, completely naked, after washing himself carefully with a piece of scented soap, he set it on the top of his head, which was shaved like ours, bent forward and, with imperceptible practiced and precise undulations of his back, made the luxurious piece of soap slide little by little from head to neck, then down, down along the entire spinal column all the way to his coccyx, at which point he made it fall into his hand. Two or three of us applauded but he showed no sign of noticing and went off to dress, slowly and abstractedly.

At work he was unpredictable. Sometimes he did the work of ten men, but even in the dullest tasks he never failed to reveal, suddenly, his professional bent. He would be shoveling dirt and all of a sudden would stop, seize the shovel as if it were a guitar, and improvise a popular song, beating on it with a pebble, now on the wooden handle, now on the iron part. He would be carrying bricks and returning with his dancing, dreamy gait,

and all at once he would roll into a fast somersault.
Other days he remained huddled in a corner without
lifting a finger, but precisely because he was capable of
such extraordinary feats no one dared say anything to
him. He was not an exhibitionist; doing his tricks he did
not pay the least attention to those around him. He
seemed instead to be preoccupied with the perfection of
his performances, repeating and improving them, like a
dissatisfied poet who never stops correcting his work. At
times we saw him hunting through the scrap metal
strewn around the workyard, picking up a hoop, a rod, a
snippet of sheet metal, turning it attentively in his hands,
balancing it on one finger, whirling it through the air, as
though he were trying to penetrate its essence and build
a new trick around it.

One day a wagon arrived full of cardboard tubes,
like the ones used for rolls of cloth, and our work-squad
was sent to unload them. Eddy took me into an under-
ground storeroom, where, below a small window, he set
up a wooden chute to be used by my companions for
sending down the tubes. He showed me how I had to
pile them neatly against the walls, and left. From the
little window I could see my companions, happy because
of the unusually light work but uncertain and clumsy in
their movements, shuttling between wagon and storeroom, carrying twenty or thirty tubes a trip. Eddy carried
a few at times and a lot at others, but never haphazardly.
Every time he made the circuit he invented new struc-
tures and architectures, unsteady but symmetrical as card

30   castles. On one trip he tossed four or five tubes in the air, the way jugglers do with rubber balls.

I was alone in the cellar, anxious to carry through an important operation. I had gotten hold of a sheet of paper and a pencil stub, and for many days I had been waiting for the opportunity to write the draft of a letter (in Italian, of course) which I meant to entrust to an Italian "free" laborer so he could copy it, sign it as if it were his, and send it to my family in Italy. In fact we were strictly forbidden to write, but I was sure that if I could think about it for a moment, I would find a way to devise a message that would be sufficiently clear to the recipients but at the same time innocent enough not to attract the censor's attention. I could not risk being seen by anyone because the fact of writing alone was intrinsically suspect (for what reason and to whom should one of us be writing?), and the Camp and the workyard teemed with informers. After not quite an hour of work on the tubes I felt calm enough to begin writing the letter. The tubes descended from the chute at infrequent intervals, and there was no alarming sound in the cellar.

I hadn't reckoned with Eddy's noiseless step. I noticed him only when he was already watching me. Instinctively—or, rather, stupidly—I opened my fingers. The pencil fell, and the sheet of paper descended slowly to the ground, swaying like a dead leaf. Eddy lunged to pick it up, then slammed me to the ground with a violent slap. But there: as I write this sentence today, and as I am in the act of typing the word "slap," I realize that I am lying, or at least transmitting biased emotions and information to the reader. Eddy was not a brute; he did not mean to punish me or make me suffer. A slap inflicted in the Camp had a very different significance from what it might have here among us in today's here and now. Precisely: it had a meaning; it was simply another way of expressing oneself. In that context it meant roughly "Watch out, you've really made a big mistake this time, you're endangering your life, maybe without realizing it, and you're endangering mine as well." But between Eddy, a German thief and juggler, and me, a young, inexperienced Italian, flustered and confused, such a speech would have been useless, not understood (if nothing else, because of language problems), out of tune, and much too roundabout.

For this very reason, punches and slaps passed among us as daily language, and we soon learned to distinguish meaningful blows from the others inflicted out of savagery, to create pain and humiliation, and which often resulted in death. A slap like Eddy's was akin to the friendly smack you give a dog, or the whack you administer to a donkey to convey or reinforce an order or prohibition. Nothing more in short than a nonverbal communication. Among the many miseries in the Camp, blows of this nature were by far the least painful. Which is equivalent to saying that our manner of living was not very different from that of donkeys and dogs.

Eddy waited for me to get up, then asked to whom I was writing. I answered in my bad German that I was not writing to anyone. I happened to find a pencil and was writing on a whim, out of nostalgia, in a dream. Yes,

32   I knew very well that writing was forbidden, but I also
knew that getting a letter out of the Camp was impossible; I assured him I never would have dared to break
Camp rules. I knew Eddy certainly would not believe me
but I had to say something, if only to arouse his pity. If
he were to denounce me to the Political Section, I knew
it was the gallows for me, but before the gallows an interrogation—and what an interrogation!—to find out who
my accomplice was, and perhaps also to obtain from me
the address of the recipient in Italy. Eddy looked at me
with a strange expression, then told me not to budge,
he'd be back in an hour.

It was a long hour. Eddy came back to the cellar
with three sheets of paper in his hand, mine among
them, and I immediately read on his face that the worst
would not happen. He must have been quite clever, this
Eddy, or maybe his tempestuous past had taught him the
basics of the sad profession of interrogator. He had looked
among my companions for two men (not just one) who
knew both German and Italian, and had gotten them
separately to translate my message into German, warning them that if the two translations did not turn out to
be identical, he would denounce not only me but also
them to the Political Section.

He made a speech to me that I find difficult to repeat. He told me that, luckily for me, the two translations were the same and the text was not compromising.
That I was crazy—there was no other explanation. Only
a madman would think of gambling in such a way with
his life, that of the Italian accomplice whom I certainly

had, my relatives in Italy, and also his career as Kapo. He told me that I deserved that slap, that in fact I should thank him because it had been a good deed, the kind that earns you Paradise, and that he, *Strassenräuber*, a street-thief by profession, certainly needed to perform good deeds. That, finally, he would not have recourse to denunciation but even he could not exactly say why. Maybe just because I *was* crazy. But then Italians are all notoriously crazy, good only for singing and getting into trouble.

I don't believe I thanked Eddy, but from that day on, even though I felt no positive attraction to my green triangle "colleagues," I often asked myself what kind of humanity was massed behind their symbol, and I have regretted that none of their ambiguous brigade has, so far as I know, told his story. I don't know how Eddy ended up. A few weeks after this incident he disappeared for several days; then we saw him one evening. He was standing in the passage between the barbed wire and the electrified fence, and around his neck hung a sign on which was written *Urning* (pederast), but he appeared neither upset nor anxious. He watched the re-entry of our work-group with a distracted, insolent, and lazy look, as though nothing that was happening around him concerned him in the slightest.

Lilith

IN THE SPACE of a few minutes the sky had turned black and it began to rain. Soon the rain increased until it became a stubborn downpour and the thick earth of the workyard changed to a blanket of mud, a handsbreadth deep. It was impossible not only to go on shoveling but even to stand up. Our Kapo questioned the civilian foreman, then turned to us: we should all go and take shelter wherever we could. Scattered about there were various sections of iron pipe, about seventeen to eighteen feet long and over a yard in diameter. I crawled into one of these and halfway down it I met the Tischler, who had had the same idea and had come in from the other end.

Tischler means carpenter, and this was the only name by which he was known to us. There were also the Blacksmith, the Russian, the Fool, two Tailors (respectively the Tailor and the Other Tailor), the Galician,

38   and the Tall Man. For a long time I was the Italian, then, indiscriminately, Primo or Alberto, because they mixed me up with another Italian.

So the Tischler was Tischler and nothing more, but he didn't look like a carpenter and we all suspected that he was no such thing. In those days it was common practice for an engineer to register as a mechanic, or a journalist to put himself down as a typographer. Thus one could hope to get better work than that of a common laborer without unleashing the Nazi wrath against intellectuals. At any rate, Tischler had been placed at the carpenters' bench and his carpentry was pretty good. An unusual thing for a Polish Jew, he spoke a little Italian. It had been taught him by his father, who had been captured by the Italians in 1917 and taken to a camp—a concentration camp, in fact—somewhere near Turin. Most of his father's comrades had died of Spanish influenza. You can still, as a matter of fact, read their exotic names today, Hungarian, Polish, Croat and German names, on a columbarium in the Cimitero Maggiore. That visit fills the visitor with pain at the thought of those forlorn deaths. Tischler's father caught the flu too, but recovered.

Tischler's Italian was amusing and full of errors, consisting principally of scraps from librettos of operas, his father having been a great opera buff. Often at work I had heard him singing arias: "*sconto col sangue mio*" and "*libiamo nei lieti calici.*" His mother tongue was Yiddish but he also spoke German and we had no trouble understanding each other. I liked Tischler because he never succumbed to lethargy. His step was brisk in

spite of his wooden clogs, his speech was careful and
precise, and he had an alert face, laughing and sad. Sometimes in the evening he staged entertainments in Yiddish, telling little anecdotes and reciting long strings of
verses, and I was sorry I couldn't understand him. Sometimes he also sang, and then nobody clapped and everyone stared at the ground, but when he was through they
begged him to start again.

That almost canine encounter of ours on all fours
cheered him up. If only it rained like that every day! But
this was a special day: the rain had come for him because
it was his birthday: twenty-five years old. Now, by sheer
chance I was twenty-five that day too; we were twins.
Tischler said it was a date that called for a celebration
since it was most unlikely that we would celebrate our
next birthday. He took half an apple out of his pocket,
cut off a slice, and made me a present of it, and that was
the only time in a year of imprisonment that I tasted
fruit.

We chewed in silence, as attentive to the precious
acidulous flavor as we would have been to a symphony.
In the meantime, in the pipe opposite ours, a woman
had taken refuge. She was young, bundled up in black
rags, perhaps a Ukrainian belonging to the Todt Organization, which consisted of "volunteer" (they had little
or no choice) foreign laborers recruited for war work.
She had a broad red face, glistening with rain, and she
looked at us and laughed. She scratched herself with provocative indolence under her jacket, then undid her hair,
combed it unhurriedly, and began braiding it again. In

40 those days it rarely happened that one saw a woman
close up, an experience both tender and savage that left
you shattered.

Tischler noticed that I was staring at her and asked
if I was married. No, I wasn't. He looked at me with
mock severity: to be celibate at our age was a sin. However, he turned around and stayed that way for some
time, looking at the girl. She had finished braiding her
hair, had crouched down in her pipe, and was humming,
swaying her head in time with the music.

"It's Lilith," Tischler suddenly said to me.

"You know her? Is that her name?"

"I don't know her but I recognize her. She's Lilith,
Adam's first wife. Don't you know the story of Lilith?"

I didn't know it and he laughed indulgently: everyone knows that western Jews are all Epicureans—*apicor-
sim,* unbelievers. Then he continued: "If you had read
the Bible carefully, you would remember that the business of the creation of woman is told twice, in two different ways. But you people—they teach you a little Hebrew
when you reach thirteen and that's the end of it."

A typical situation was developing, and a game that
I liked: the dispute between the pious man and the unbeliever who is by definition ignorant, and whom the
adversary forces to gnash his teeth by showing him his
error. I accepted my role and answered with the required
insolence.

"Yes, it's told twice but the second time is only the
commentary on the first."

"Wrong. That's the way the man who doesn't probe

below the surface understands it. Look: if you read attentively and reason about what you're reading, you'll realize
that in the first account it says only: "God created them
male and female." That is to say, He created them equal,
with the same dust. However, it says on the next page
that God forms Adam, then decides it isn't good for man
to be alone, takes one of Adam's ribs, and with the rib
He fashions a woman, actually a *Männin*, a she-man.
You see that here equality is gone. There are even people
who believe that not only the two stories but the two
women are different, and that the first wasn't Eve, man's
rib, but Lilith. Now the story of Eve is written down and
everybody knows it; the story of Lilith, instead, is only
told, so that few know it—know the stories, actually,
because there are many. I'll tell you a few of them,
because it's our birthday and it's raining, and because
today my role is to tell and believe; you are the unbeliever today.

"The first story is that the Lord not only made man
and woman equal, but He made a single form out of
clay—in fact a Golem, a form without form, a two-backed
figure: that is, man and woman already joined together.
Then He separated them with one cut but they were
anxious to be joined again, and right away Adam wanted
Lilith to lie down on the ground. Lilith wouldn't hear
of it: 'Why should I be underneath? Aren't we equal?
Two halves made of the same stuff?' Adam tried to
force her to, but they were also equal in strength and
he did not succeed. So he asked God for help: He was
male too and would say Adam was right. And so He

42 did, but Lilith rebelled: equal rights or nothing, and since the two males persisted, she cursed the Lord's name, became a she-devil, flew off like an arrow and went to live at the bottom of the sea. Some even claim to know more and say that Lilith lives in the Red Sea, precisely. But every night she rises in flight, wanders around the world, rustles against the windows of houses where there are newborn babies, and tries to smother them. You have to watch out: if she gets in, she must be caught under an overturned bowl. Then she can no longer do any harm.

"At other times she enters the body of a man, and the man becomes possessed. And then the best remedy is to take him before a notary or a rabbinical tribunal, and draw up a deed in due form in which the man declares that he wants to repudiate the she-devil. Why are you laughing? Of course, I don't believe this, but I like to tell these stories. I liked it when they were told to me, and it would be a shame if they were lost. In any case, I won't guarantee that I myself didn't add something, and perhaps all who tell them add something: and that's how stories are born."

We heard a distant racket and shortly afterwards a Caterpillar-tread tractor passed alongside us. It was dragging a snowplow. But the mud it cleaved immediately joined together again behind the machine. Like Adam and Lilith, I thought to myself. Better for us; we would continue to rest for quite a while.

"Then there's the story of the seed. Lilith is greedy for man's seed, and she is always lying in wait wherever

it may get spilled, especially between the sheets. All the
seed that doesn't end in the only approved place—that is,
inside the wife's womb—is hers: all the seed that every
man has wasted in his lifetime, in dreams or vice or
adultery. So you see she gets a lot of it and so she's always
pregnant and giving birth all the time. Being a she-
devil she gives birth to devils, but they don't do much
harm even if they would perhaps like to. They're evil
little spirits, without bodies. They make milk and wine
turn, run about attics at night, and snarl girls' hair.

"But they are also the sons of man, of every man:
illegitimate, it's true, and when their fathers die they
come to the funeral along with the legitimate sons who
are their half-brothers. They flutter around the funeral
candles like nocturnal butterflies, screech, and claim their
share of the inheritance. You laugh precisely because
you're an unbeliever and it's your role to laugh. Or perhaps you never did spill your seed. It may even happen
that you will get out of here alive. Then you'll see that at
certain funerals the rabbi and his followers circle the
dead man seven times. That's it: they are putting up a
barrier so that his bodiless sons will not come to give him
grief.

"But I still have to tell you the strangest story of all,
and it's not strange that it's strange because it's written
down in the books of the cabalists, and they were people
without fear. You know that God created Adam, and
immediately afterwards He realized it wasn't good for
man to be alone and He placed a companion at his side.
Well, the cabalists said that it wasn't good even for God

44   Himself to be alone, and so from the beginning, He took as His companion the *Shekhina*, which is to say, His own presence in the Creation. Thus the *Shekhina* became the wife of God and therefore the mother of all peoples. When the Temple in Jerusalem was destroyed by the Romans and we were dispersed and enslaved, the *Shekhina* was angered, left God, and came with us into exile. Actually I myself have thought this: that the *Shekhina* also let herself be enslaved and is here around us, in this exile within exile, in this home of mud and sorrow.

"So God has remained alone; as happens to many, He has not been able to endure solitude and resist temptation and has taken a mistress. Do you know who? Her, Lilith, the she-devil, and that was an unimaginable scandal. It seems, in short, that things unfolded as in a quarrel when one insult is answered by a more serious insult, so the quarrel never ends; on the contrary it grows like an avalanche. Because you must know that this obscene tryst has not ended, and won't end soon. In one way it's the cause of the evil that occurs on earth; in another way, it is its effect. As long as God continues to sin with Lilith, there will be blood and trouble on Earth. But one day a powerful being will come—the one we are all waiting for. He will make Lilith die and put an end to God's lechery, and to our exile. Yes, even to yours and mine, Italian. *Mazel tov*. Good fortune."

Fortune has been good enough to me but not to Tischler. And it happened many years later that I actually attended a funeral that took place exactly in the way he had described, with the protective dance around

the coffin. It is inexplicable that fate has chosen an un- 45
believer to repeat this pious and impious tale, woven of
poetry, ignorance, daring acumen, and the unassuageable
sadness that grows on the ruins of lost civilizations.

A Disciple

THE HUNGARIANS arrived among us, not in a trickle but all at once. In the space of two months, May and June 1944, they invaded the Camp, convoy after convoy, filling the void which the Germans had not neglected to create with a series of diligent selections. The newcomers caused a profound change in the fabric of all the Camps. At Auschwitz the wave of Magyars reduced the other nationalities to minorities, without, however, making a dent in the cadres, which remained in the hands of the German and Polish common criminals.

All the barracks and work-squads were inundated by the Hungarians, around whom, as happens in all communities around new arrivals, an atmosphere of derision, gossip, and vague intolerance rapidly condensed. They were workmen and peasants, simple and robust, who did not fear manual labor but were used to abundant food, and who, for that reason, in a few weeks were reduced to

50   pitiful skeletons. Others were professional men, students and intellectuals, who came from Budapest or other cities. They were mild individuals, slow, patient, and methodical, and hunger afflicted them less, but they had delicate skins, and in no time at all were covered with sores and bruises, like ill-treated horses.

At the end of June a good half of my squad was made up of fine fellows, still well nourished, still full of optimism and joviality. They communicated with us in a curious dragged-out German, and communicated with each other in their odd language, which bristles with unusual inflections, and seems to be made up of interminable words, pronounced with irritating slowness, and all with the accent on the first syllable.

One of them was assigned to me as work companion. He was a strong, pink-faced young man, of medium height, whom everyone called Bandi: the diminutive of Endre—Andrew—he explained to me as though it were the most natural thing in the world. Our task that day was to carry bricks on a sort of crude wooden litter equipped with two poles in front and two behind: twenty bricks a trip. Halfway along the path stood an overseer, and he checked to see that the load was regulation.

Twenty bricks are heavy; so on the outgoing trip we did not have much breath, or at least I didn't, for talking; but on the way back we spoke and I learned many attractive things about Bandi. I wouldn't be able to repeat them all today: every memory fades. And yet I cling to the memories of this man Bandi as precious things, and I am happy to preserve them on a page. I only wish that, by some not-impossible miracle, the page might reach him in the corner of the world where he still lives, perhaps, that he might read it and recognize himself in it.

He told me his name was Endre Szántó, a name which is pronounced more or less like *santo* in Italian, and this reinforced in me the vague impression that a halo seemed to encircle his shaved head. I told him so; but no, he explained laughingly to me: Szántó means plowman, or, more generically, peasant. It is a very common last name in Hungary, and besides, he was not a plowman but worked in a factory. The Germans had captured him three years earlier, not because he was Jewish but because of his political activity, had enrolled him in the Todt Organization and sent him to be a woodcutter in the Ukrainian Carpathians. He had spent two winters in the woods, cutting down pine trees with three companions: heavy work but he had liked it and had been almost happy there. Besides, I soon realized that Bandi had a unique talent for happiness. Oppression, humiliation, hard work, exile—all seemed to slide off him like water off a rock, without corrupting or wounding him, indeed purifying and enhancing in him his inborn capacity for joy, as we are told happened to the simple, cheerful, and pious Chassidim described by Jirí Langer in his novel *The Nine Doors*.

Bandi told me about his entrance into the Camp. When the convoy arrived, the SS forced all the men to take off their shoes and hang them around their necks, and then made them walk barefoot on the jagged stones

52 of the railroad bed for the entire seven kilometers that separated the station from the Camp. He recounted the episode with a shy smile, without asking for commiseration; on the contrary with a touch of childlike and athletic vanity for having "brought it off."

We made three trips together, during which I tried, in a fragmentary fashion, to explain to him that the place he had landed in was not for polite or quiet people. I tried to convince him of a few recent discoveries of mine (in truth, not yet well digested): that down there, in order to get by, it was necessary to get busy, organize illegal food, dodge work, find influential friends, hide one's thoughts, steal, and lie; that whoever did not do so was soon dead, and that his saintliness seemed dangerous to me and out of place. And since, as I have said, twenty bricks are heavy, on our fourth trip, instead of taking twenty of them off the wagon, I took seventeen and showed him that if you placed them on the litter in a certain way, with an empty space in the lower layer, no one would ever suspect that there weren't twenty. This was a ruse I thought I had invented (I found out later that it was, however, in the public domain), and that I had used several times with success. At other times it had earned me some nasty blows. In any case, it seemed to me that for pedagogical purposes it served well as an illustration of the theories I had expounded to him just before.

Bandi was very sensitive about his condition of "*Zugang*," that is, new arrival, and to the condition of social subjection that derived from it. Therefore he did

not object, but neither did he show any enthusiasm for
my invention. "If there are seventeen, why should we
make them believe that there are twenty?"

"But twenty bricks weigh more than seventeen," I
answered impatiently, "and if they're well arranged, no
one will notice. Besides, they're not going to be used to
build your house or mine."

"Yes," he said, "but they're still seventeen bricks
and not twenty." He was not a good disciple.

We worked together for a few more weeks in the
same squad. He told me that he was a Communist sym-
pathizer, not a Party member, but his language was that
of a proto-Christian. At work he was dexterous and
strong, the best worker in the squad, but he did not try
to profit from this superiority of his, or show off to the
German foremen, or lord it over us. I told him that in my
opinion working like this was a waste of energy, and that
it was also politically wrong, but Bandi gave no sign of
understanding me; he did not want to lie. In that place
we were supposed to work; so he worked as best he could.
In no time, with his radiant and childlike face, his energetic voice and awkward gait, Bandi became very popular, everybody's friend.

August came, with an extraordinary gift for me: a
letter from home—an unprecedented event. In June, with
frightful irresponsibility, and through the mediation of a
"free" Italian laborer who was a bricklayer, I had written
a message for my mother, who was hidden in Italy, and
addressed it to a woman friend of mine named Bianca
Guidetti Serra. I had done all this as one observes a

54 ritual, without really hoping for success. Instead, my letter had arrived without difficulty, and my mother had answered via the same route. The letter from the sweet world burned in my pocket; I knew that it was elementary prudence to keep silent, and yet I had to talk about it.

At that time we were cleaning cisterns. I went down into my cistern and Bandi was with me. By the weak gleam of the light bulb, I read the miraculous letter, hastily translating it into German. Bandi listened attentively. Certainly he could not understand much because German was neither my language nor his, and also because the message was scant and reticent. But he understood what was essential for him to understand: that that piece of paper in my hands, which had reached me in such a precarious way and which I would destroy before nightfall, represented a breach, a small gap in the black universe that closed tightly around us, and through that breach hope could pass. At least I believe that Bandi, even though he was a *Zugang*, understood or sensed all this, because when I was through reading he came close to me, rummaged at length in his pocket, and finally, with loving care, pulled out a radish. He gave it to me, blushing deeply, and said with shy pride: "I've learned. This is for you. It's the first thing I've stolen."

Our Seal

THIS IS HOW things go here in the morning: when reveille sounds (and it's still pitch dark) first of all we put on our shoes, otherwise somebody will steal them and it is an unspeakable tragedy. Then, in the dust and crush, we try to make our beds according to regulations. Immediately after that, we rush to the latrines and the washroom, run to get on line for bread, and finally we make a dash to the roll-call square. We join our work-squads and wait for the head-count to end and the sky to grow lighter. One by one in the dark, the ghosts who are our companions approach. Our squad is a good one; we have a certain esprit de corps; there are no clumsy or whining rookies and among us exists a rough friendship. In the morning it is customary for us to greet one another formally: good morning Herr Doctor, good day Signor Lawyer, how was your night Mr. President? Did you enjoy breakfast?

58   Lomnitz showed up, the antiquarian from Frankfurt, then Joulty, a mathematician from Paris; next
Hirsch, a mysterious businessman from Copenhagen,
Janek the Aryan, a huge railroad worker from Cracow,
and Elias, the dwarf from Warsaw, uncouth, crazy, and
probably a spy. Last, as always, came Wolf, the Berlin
pharmacist, bent like a hook, wearing glasses, and mewl-
ing a musical theme. His Jewish nose cleaved the murky
air like a ship's prow. He called it *"hutménu,"* Hebrew
for "our seal."

     "Here comes the sorcerer, the anointer of scabies,"
Elias announced ceremoniously. "Welcome to our midst,
Most Illustrious Excellency, *Hochwohlgeborener.* Did
you sleep well? What news did the night bring? Is Hitler
dead? Have the English landed?"

     Wolf took his place in the line. His mewling stead-
ily increased in volume, its tones grew richer and more
variegated, and some of his companions recognized the
concluding measures of the Brahms Rhapsody op. 53.
Wolf, a reserved, dignified man in his forties, lived on
music: he was steeped in it; ever new themes chased each
other unceasingly through him. Others he seemed to
breathe in, drawing them from the Camp air through his
famous nose. He secreted music as our stomachs secreted
hunger: he reproduced single instruments accurately (but
without virtuosity); now he was a violin, now a flute,
now an orchestra conductor and, with a deep frown, he
conducted himself.

     Someone snickered and Wolf (Wòlef, according to

the Yiddish pronunciation) demanded silence with an
irritated gesture: he wasn't finished yet. He sang with
great concentration, bent forward, his eyes on the ground.
Soon, around him, shoulder to shoulder, a ring of four
or five companions formed, all with the same posture, as
if drawing warmth from a brazier at their feet. Wolf
went from being a violin to being a viola, repeated the
theme three times in three glorious variations, then broke
off with one final rich note. He applauded himself dis-
creetly all alone, then others joined in the applause and
Wolf bowed solemnly. The ovation ceased but Elias continued to clap violently, shouting "Wolf, Wòlef, Scabies-
wòlef. Wòlef is the smartest man of all. And do you
know why?"

Wolf, having resumed the dimensions of a common
mortal, looked at Elias with mistrust.

"How come he has scabies and doesn't scratch!"
said Elias. "This is a miracle: blessed be Thou, the Lord
our God, King of the Universe. I know them, I know
these Prussians: the Dean of the camp Prussian, the doctor who treats scabies Prussian. Wolf is Prussian, and
sure enough Wolf becomes an anointer and then Scabieswolf. But no doubt about it: he's a wonderful anointer;
he smears on ointment like a Jewish mother, like a
dream. He has anointed me too, and cured me, praise be
to God and to all the Just. Now, by dint of anointing
everybody, he too has caught scabies and anoints himself.
Isn't that true, Maestro? Oh yes, he anoints his belly,
because that's where it starts. He does it on the sly every

60 evening. I've seen him; nothing escapes me. However, he's a strong character: he doesn't scratch. The Just don't scratch themselves."

"Nonsense," said Janek the Aryan. "Anybody who's got the mange scratches. Mange is like being in love; if you've got it, it shows."

"Sure. But Maestro Mangywolf has it and doesn't scratch. Didn't I say he's the smartest man of all?"

"Elias, you're a liar, the biggest liar in this Camp. It's impossible to have scabies and not scratch." As he said this, Janek began to scratch himself without being aware of it, and little by little the others too began to scratch. In any case, all of us had scabies, were about to get it, or had just recovered from it. Elias pointed out Janek to the gathering with an ogreish laugh: "There, just look if Wòlef isn't made of iron. Even the healthy ones scratch themselves, and Wolf, who is covered with mange, stands there stock-still, like a king." Then with a sudden spring he threw himself on Wolf, pulled down his pants and lifted his shirt. In the uncertain light of dawn we glimpsed Wolf's belly, pale and shriveled, covered with scratches and inflamed spots. Wolf jumped back, trying at the same time to ward off Elias, but the latter, who was a head shorter, leaped up and clung to Wolf's neck. Both men collapsed to the ground in the black mud, Elias on top and Wolf gasping, half suffocated. Some tried to intervene, but Elias was strong and he clung to the other man with his arms and legs, like an octopus. Wolf's defense grew weaker and weaker as he

tried to rain blows blindly on Elias with his feet and
knees.

Luckily for Wolf, the Kapo arrived, dealt out kicks
and punches, Solomon-fashion, to the two men entan-
gled on the ground, separated them, and lined everyone
up: it was time to march off to work. The incident was
not particularly memorable, and indeed was soon forgotten, but the nickname Scabieswolf (*Krätzewolf*) tena-
ciously stuck to the protagonist, a crack flawing his re-
spectability even many months after he was cured of
scabies and relieved of the position of anointer. He did
not take it well and visibly suffered from it, thus helping
to keep it from fading away.

A timid spring at last arrived, and in one of the first
stretches of sunshine there was a work-free Sunday afternoon, fragile and precious as a peach blossom. Everybody
spent the day sleeping, the more energetic exchanging
visits between barracks, or trying to mend their rags, at-
tach buttons with wire, or file their nails on a stone. But
from far away, carried by the whims of a tepid wind
redolent of damp earth, we heard a new sound, a sound
so improbable, so unexpected, that everyone lifted his
head to listen. The sound was frail, like that sky and that
sun. True, it came from far away, but from within the
boundaries of the Camp. Some overcame their inertia and
set out to search, like bloodhounds, running into one another with faltering steps, their ears pricked, and they
found Mangywolf sitting on a pile of boards, ecstatic,
playing a violin. His "seal"—lifted to the sun—was quiver-

62 ing, his myopic gaze lost somewhere beyond the barbed wire, beyond the pale Polish sky. Where he could have found a violin was a mystery, but the veterans knew that in a Camp anything can happen. Perhaps he had stolen it; perhaps rented it in exchange for bread.

Wolf played for himself, but all those who came by stopped to listen with a greedy look, like bears catching the scent of honey, avid, timid, and perplexed. A few steps away lay Elias, his belly on the ground, staring at Wolf, almost spellbound. On his gladiator's face hovered that veil of contented stupor one sometimes sees on the faces of the dead, that makes one think they really had for an instant, on the threshold, the vision of a better world.

The Gypsy

A NOTICE WAS AFFIXED to the door of the barracks and everyone jostled to read it. It was written in German and Polish, and a French prisoner, caught between the crowd and the wooden wall, laboriously tried to translate and comment on it. The notice said that as a special exception, all prisoners were to be allowed to write to their relatives under conditions that were minutely spelled out, in true German fashion. You could write only on forms that each barracks-chief would distribute, one to a prisoner. The only permissible language was German, and the only approved addressees were those who lived in Germany, or in the occupied territories, or in allied countries like Italy. You were not allowed to ask for food packages to be sent but it was all right to thank people for any packages you might possibly receive. At this point the Frenchman exclaimed forcefully: "The bastards!" and broke off.

66   The din and pushing and shoving got worse and there was a confused exchange of opinions in several languages. Who had ever officially received a package? Or even only a letter? Besides, who knew our address, if "KZ Auschwitz" could be considered an address? And to whom could we write, since all our relatives were like us imprisoned in some Camp, or dead, or in hiding here and there in every corner of Europe, in terror of suffering the same fate as ours? Obviously it was a trick: the thank-you letters with the Auschwitz postal mark would be shown to the Red Cross delegation, or who knows what other neutral authority, to prove that after all the Jews in Auschwitz were not treated all that badly, seeing as how they received packages from home. A filthy lie.

Three opinions were formed: not to write at all, to write without thanking anyone, to write and thank. The partisans of this last course of action (few, to be sure) maintained that the theory of the Red Cross was likely but not certain, and there still existed a probability— however slight—that the letters would reach their destinations and the thanks would be interpreted as a suggestion to send packages. I decided to write without thanking, addressing the letter to Christian friends who somehow would find my family. I borrowed a pencil-stub, obtained the form, and set to work. I first wrote a draft on a scrap of cement wrapper which I wore (illegally) on my chest to protect myself from the wind, then I began to copy the text onto the form, but I felt ill at ease. For the first time since my capture I felt in com-

munication and communion (albeit only theoretically) 67
with my family, and so I would have liked solitude. But
solitude in a Camp is more precious and rare than bread.

I had the irksome impression that someone was
watching me. I turned around: it was my new bunkmate.
He quietly watched me write with the innocent but
provocative fixity of children, who feel no shame about
staring. He had arrived a few weeks earlier with a train-
load of Hungarians and Slovaks; he was very young, slim
and dark. I knew nothing about him, not even his name,
because he was in a different squad and got into the
bunk to sleep only at curfew.

There was little feeling of *camaraderie* among us. It
was confined to compatriots, and even toward them it
was weakened by the minimal life conditions. It was actually zero, indeed negative, with regard to newcomers.
In this and many other respects we had greatly retro-
gressed and become hardened. And in the "new" fellow
prisoner we tended to see an alien, an oafish, cumbersome barbarian who took up space, time, and bread, who
did not know the unspoken but ironclad rules of coexis-
tence and survival, and who, moreover, complained (and
for the wrong reasons) in an irritating and ridiculous
manner because just a few days back he was still at home,
or at least outside the barbed wire. The new arrival has
only one virtue; he brings recent news from the world,
because he's read the newspapers and listened to the
radio—perhaps even the Allied radio broadcasts; but if
the news he brings is bad, for example that the war will

68   not end in two weeks, then he is nothing but a nuisance, to be shunned or derided for his ignorance, or subjected to cruel jokes.

That newcomer behind me, however, although he was spying on me, aroused in me a vague feeling of compassion. He seemed defenseless and disoriented, in need of support, like a child; certainly he had not grasped the importance of the choice to be made, whether to write and what to write, and he was neither tense nor suspicious. I turned my back to him, to prevent him from seeing my sheet of paper, and went on with my work, which wasn't easy. It was a matter of weighing each word so that it would convey the maximum of information to the improbable recipient and, at the same time, would not appear suspect to the probable censor. Having to write in German added to the difficulty: I had gotten my German in the Camp, and, without my realizing it, it reproduced the drab, vulgar barracks jargon. I did not know many terms, exactly those needed to express feelings. I felt inept, as if I had to carve that letter in stone.

My bunkmate patiently waited until I was finished, then he said something in a language I did not understand. I asked him in German what he wanted, and he showed me his form, which was blank, and pointed to mine, which was covered with writing. In short, he was asking me to write for him. He must have understood that I was Italian, and to better clarify his request, he delivered a muddled speech in slapdash language that was in fact more Spanish than Italian. Not only did he not know how to write in German; he didn't know how to write at all. He was a gypsy, had been born in Spain, and had wandered about in Germany, Austria, and the Balkans, only to end up in the Nazis' dragnets in Hungary. He introduced himself formally: Grigo, his name was Grigo, he was nineteen, and he begged me to write to his fiancée. He would pay me. With what? A gift, he answered without specifying. I asked him for bread; half a ration seemed to me a fair price. Today I am a little ashamed of this request of mine, but I must remind the reader (and myself) that Auschwitz etiquette was different from ours. And besides, Grigo, having arrived a short while before, was less hungry than I.

And he did accept. I reached out for his form but he pulled it away and instead handed me another scrap of paper: it was an important letter, better to make a draft. He began to dictate the girl's address. He must have caught a blink of curiosity or perhaps envy in my eyes because he pulled a photograph from his shirt and showed it to me with pride: she was almost a child, with laughing eyes, a little white kitten by her side. My respect for the gypsy increased; it was not easy to enter the Camp with a hidden photograph. Almost as though he felt a justification was needed, Grigo specified that she had not been picked by him but by his father. She was an official fiancée, not a girl abducted unceremoniously.

The letter which he dictated to me was a complicated love letter, full of domestic details. It contained questions the sense of which escaped me, and information about the Camp which I advised Grigo to omit because it was too compromising. On one point Grigo in-

70 sisted: he wanted to announce to the girl that he was going to send her a *"muñeca."* A *muñeca?* Yes, a doll, Grigo explained as best he could. I found this embarrassing for two reasons: because I did not know how to say "doll" in German, and because I could not imagine for what reason and in what way Grigo wanted to or had to commit himself to this insane and dangerous undertaking. I felt it my duty to explain all this to him. I had more experience than he, and it seemed to me that my role as scribe imposed certain obligations.

Grigo bestowed on me a disarming smile, a "newcomer's" smile, but did not explain much, I don't know whether because of his inability, or because of the linguistic conflict, or with deliberate intention. He told me that he absolutely must send the doll, that finding it was no problem: he would fabricate it on the spot, right there, and he showed me a pretty little pocketknife. No, this Grigo definitely knew his way around. Once again I was forced to admire him. He must have been very ingenious when he entered the Camp, when they take away everything you have on you, even your handkerchief and hair. Perhaps he didn't realize it but a knife like his was worth at least five rations of bread.

He asked me to tell him if there was a tree somewhere from which he could cut a branch, because it was better if the doll was made *de madera viva*—of live wood. Again I tried to dissuade him, descending to his level: there were no trees, and besides, sending the girl a doll made of Auschwitz wood, wasn't it like attracting her here? But Grigo lifted his eyebrows with a mysterious air, touched his nose with his index finger, and said that if anything it was exactly the contrary: the doll would pull him out, the girl knew what to do.

When the letter was finished, Grigo pulled out a ration of bread and handed it to me together with the knife. It was the custom, indeed the unwritten law, that in all payments based on bread one of the contracting parties must cut the bread and the other choose, because in this way the person who cuts is induced to make the portions as equal as possible. I was surprised that Grigo already knew the rule, but then I thought that perhaps it applied also outside the Camp, in the to me unknown world from which Grigo came. I cut, and he praised me gallantly. That both half rations were the same was to his disadvantage but I had cut well, no doubt about that. He thanked me and I never saw him again. Needless to say, none of the letters we wrote that day ever reached its destination.

The Cantor
and the Barracks Chief

THE NEW BARRACKS CHIEF was German, but he spoke with a dialect accent that made what he said hard to understand. He was about fifty, tall, muscular and corpulent. Rumor had it that he belonged to the old-guard German Communist Party, that he had taken part in the Spartacus revolt and been wounded in it, but, since the Camp swarmed with spies, this was not a subject one could talk about openly. He did have a scar which cut across his blondish, bushy eyebrows, and he was certainly a veteran. He had been in the Camp for seven years, and under the red triangle of the political prisoner he proudly wore an incredibly low registration number: Number 14.

Before Auschwitz he had been at Dachau, and at Auschwitz he had been one of the founding fathers. He had belonged to the legendary patrol of thirty prisoners who had been sent from Dachau to the marshes of Upper Silesia to build the first barracks. He was, in short, one

76 of those who, in all human communities, claim the right to say "in my day" and feel entitled therefore to be respected. And respected he was, not so much for his past as for his heavy fists and still very quick reflexes. His name was Otto.

Now Vladek never washed. The fact was notorious, and was the subject of jokes and gossip in the barracks. But it was quite comic because Vladek was not Jewish; he was a Polish country boy who received packages from home with fatback, fruit, and woolen socks, so he was potentially a person of some standing. All the same, he never washed.

Bony and clumsy, as soon as he returned from work Vladek burrowed into his bunk without a word to anyone. The fact is that Vladek had no more brains than a chicken, poor thing, and if, as mentioned, he hadn't enjoyed the privilege of receiving packages (the contents of which were mostly stolen from him), he would have ended in the gas chambers a long time ago, even though he too wore the political prisoners' red triangle. Our Vladek must have been some politico!

Otto had called him to order several times (because the barracks chief is responsible for the cleanliness of his subjects): first in a nice way, that is to say with insults shouted in his dialect, then with slaps and punches, but in vain. From all appearances, Vladek (who in any case understood little German) was unable to connect cause and effect, or perhaps didn't remember the blows from one day to the next.

There came a mild September Sunday, one of the

rare work-free Sundays, and Otto let it be known that there would be a celebration, a spectacle never seen before, which he was offering free of charge to all the tenants of Barracks 48—the public washing of Vladek.

One of the soup tubs was taken outside and summarily rinsed, then filled with hot water from the showers. He put Vladek in it, naked and standing up, and personally washed him as you would wash a horse, scrubbing him from head to foot, first with a heavy brush, then with the floor rags.

Vladek, who was covered with bruises and abrasions, stood there like a pole, his eyes glazed. The audience writhed with laughter, and Otto, frowning as if he were performing a task of great precision, addressed Vladek with the coarse shouts which as a matter of fact blacksmiths use with horses to stop them from shifting about while they're being shod. It really was a comic sight, enough to take one's mind off hunger, and worth describing to friends in the other barracks. In the end, Otto lifted Vladek bodily out of the tub and mumbled something in his dialect about the "gruel" that was left in the tub. Vladek was so clean that he had changed color and it would be difficult to recognize him.

We went away, concluding that this Otto was not one of the worst; another in his place would have used ice-cold water or would have had Vladek transferred to the punishment camp, or he would have beaten him up, because in Camp no special leniency was accorded to imbeciles. On the contrary, they ran the risk of being ticketed officially as such and (in keeping with the national

78 German passion for labels) supplied with a white arm-
band with BLÖD—imbecile—written on it. That emblem,
especially if coupled with the red triangle, represented an
inexhaustible source of amusement for the SS.

That Otto wasn't one of the worst was soon con-
firmed. A few days later it was Yom Kippur, the Day of
Atonement and of forgiveness, but of course we worked
anyway. It is hard to say how the date had filtered
through the Camp, since the Jewish calendar is lunar and
does not coincide with the ordinary one. Perhaps some
among the more pious Jews had kept a precise count of
the passing days, or perhaps the information was brought
by one of the new arrivals, because there always were new
arrivals to fill the gaps.

On Yom Kippur eve, we got in line for our soup,
as on every other evening. In front of me stood Ezra, a
watchmaker by trade and cantor on the Sabbath in a remote Lithuanian village. From exile to exile, by paths I
would not know how to describe, he had arrived in Italy
and there had been captured. He was tall and thin, but
not stooped. His eyes, which had an Oriental slant, were
bright and lively. He rarely spoke and never raised his
voice.

When Ezra got in front of Otto, he did not hold out
his mess tin. Instead, he said: "Mister Barracks Chief,
for us today is a day of atonement and I cannot eat my
soup. I respectfully ask you to save it for me until to-
morrow evening."

Otto, who was as tall as Ezra but twice as thick-set,
had already dipped the ration of soup from the tub and

he stopped abruptly with the ladle in midair. We saw his
jaw drop slowly in one smooth movement, and his mouth
remained agape.

In all his Camp years he had never run into a prisoner who refused food. For a few moments, he was uncertain whether to laugh or slap that unknown bean-
pole—was he perhaps making fun of him, Otto? But he
didn't look the type. Otto told him to step aside and
come back to him after he had finished ladling it out.

Ezra waited patiently, then knocked at the door.
Otto let him in, then sent his courtiers and parasites out
of the room. For that interview, he wanted to be alone.
Thus relieved of his usual role, he addressed Ezra in a
somewhat less brusque voice and asked him what was
this business of atonement. Was he perhaps less hungry
on that day than on other days?

Ezra answered that certainly he was no less hungry,
that on the day of Yom Kippur he should also abstain
from work, but he knew that if he did so he would be
denounced and killed, and therefore he would work because the Law allows disobedience of almost all precepts
and prohibitions in order to save a life, one's own or another's. That nevertheless he intended to observe the
prescribed fast, from that evening until the following
evening, because he wasn't certain that this would lead
to his death.

Otto asked him what were the sins he had to atone
for, and Ezra answered that he knew about some but
perhaps he had committed others unwittingly, and that
moreover, in the opinion of some wise men, which he

80 shared, atonement and fasting were not a strictly personal matter. Probably they contributed toward obtain-
ing forgiveness from God for sins committed by others.

Otto grew more and more perplexed, torn by amaze-
ment, the desire to laugh, and still another feeling to
which he no longer could give a name and which he had
believed had died in him, killed by the years of ambiguous, savage life in the Camps and even before that by his
political militancy, which had been rigorous. In a sub-
dued voice Ezra spoke up and explained to him that exactly on that day it is customary to read the Book of the
Prophet Jonah: yes, the one who'd been swallowed by
the fish.

Jonah was a stern prophet. After the business with
the fish, he had preached repentance to the King of
Nineveh. But when the King had repented of his sins
and those of his people and published a decree that imposed a fast on all of the people in Nineveh, and even on
their livestock, Jonah had continued to suspect a trick.
He continued to argue with the Eternal, who, on His
side, was inclined to forgive; yes, forgive the people of
Nineveh, even though they were idolaters and "could not
distinguish their right hand from their left."

Otto interrupted him: "What are you trying to tell
me with this story of yours? That you're fasting for me
too? And for everybody, even for—them? Or that I
should fast too?"

Ezra answered that, unlike Jonah, he was not a
prophet but a provincial cantor. But he must insist on
asking Mister Barracks Chief for this favor: that his soup

be saved until the following evening, and also next morning's bread. But not to keep the soup warm, that was not necessary. It was all right for Otto to let it get cold.

Otto asked why, and Ezra answered that there were two good reasons for this—one sacred and one profane. In the first place (and here, perhaps unintentionally, he began to speak in a singsong and to sway a little back and forth from the waist up, as is customary when discussing ritual matters), according to some commentators it was inadvisable to make a fire or its equivalent on the Day of Atonement, even by the hand of Christians. In the second place, Camp soup tended to go sour quickly, especially when kept in a warm place. All the prisoners preferred to eat it cold rather than sour.

Otto again objected that the soup was very thin. It was in fact more water than anything else, and so it was more a question of drinking than of eating. And as he said this, he rediscovered another long lost pleasure: the heated polemics at his party meetings. Ezra explained to him that the distinction was irrelevant. On fast days one neither eats nor drinks, not even water. However, one does not incur divine punishment if one swallows food with a total volume smaller than that of a date, or liquids of a volume smaller than that which can be held between cheek and teeth. In this accounting, food and drink are not added up.

Otto muttered an incomprehensible phrase in which the word *meshuge* was repeated. (The word means crazy in Yiddish, but it is a word all Germans understand.) Still, he asked Ezra for his mess tin, filled it, and stored

82 it in the small personal locker to which he as an official was entitled, and told Ezra that he should come the next evening and pick it up. Ezra thought the ration of soup was particularly generous.

I would not have come to know the details of this interview if Ezra himself had not reported them to me, in bits and pieces, one day as we were carrying bags of cement from one storehouse to another.

Actually Ezra wasn't really *meshuge*. He was heir to an ancient, sorrowful, and strange tradition, whose core consists in holding evil in opprobrium and in "hedging about the law" so that evil may not flood through the gaps in the hedge and submerge the law itself. In the course of the millennia, around this core has become encrusted a gigantic proliferation of comments, deductions, almost maniacally subtle distinctions, and further precepts and prohibitions. And in the course of the millennia many have behaved like Ezra throughout migrations and slaughters without number. That is why the history of the Jewish people is so ancient, sorrowful, and strange.

Last Christmas
of the War

IN MORE WAYS than one, Monowitz, a part of Auschwitz, was not a typical Camp. The barrier that separated us from the world—symbolized by the double barbed-wire fence—was not hermetic, as elsewhere. Our work brought us into daily contact with people who were "free," or at least less slaves than we were: technicians, German engineers and foremen, Russian and Polish workers, English, American, French and Italian prisoners of war. Officially they were forbidden to talk to us, the pariahs of KZ (*Konzentrations-Zentrum*), but the prohibition was constantly ignored, and what's more, news from the free world reached us through a thousand channels. In the factory trash bins we found copies of the daily papers (sometimes two or three days old and rainsoaked) and in them we read with trepidation the German bulletins: mutilated, censored, euphemistic, yet eloquent. The Allied POWs listened secretly to Radio

86   London, and even more secretly brought us the news, and it was exhilarating. In December 1944 the Russians had entered Hungary and Poland, the English were in the Romagna, the Americans were heavily engaged in the Ardennes but were winning in the Pacific against Japan.

At any rate, there was no real need of news from far away to find out how the war was going. At night, when all the noises of the Camp had died down, we heard the thunder of the artillery coming closer and closer. The front was no more than a hundred kilometers away; a rumor spread that the Red Army was already in the West Carpathians. The enormous factory in which we worked had been bombed from the air several times with vicious and scientific precision: one bomb, only one, on the central power plant, putting it out of commission for two weeks; as soon as the damage was repaired and the stack began belching smoke again, another bomb and so on. It was clear that the Russians, or the Allies in concert with the Russians, intended to stop production but not destroy the plants. These they wanted to capture intact at the end of the war, as indeed they did; today that is Poland's largest synthetic rubber factory. Active anti-aircraft defense was nonexistent, no pursuing planes were to be seen; there were guns on the roofs but they didn't fire. Perhaps they no longer had ammunition.

In short, Germany was moribund, but the Germans didn't notice. After the attempt on Hitler in July, the country lived in a state of terror: a denunciation, an absence from work, an incautious word, were sufficient to land you in the hands of the Gestapo as a defeatist.

Therefore both soldiers and civilians fulfilled their tasks as usual, driven at once by fear and an innate sense of discipline. A fanatical and suicidal Germany terrorized a Germany that was by now discouraged and profoundly defeated.

A short time before, toward the end of October, we'd had the opportunity to observe a close-up of a singular school of fanaticism, a typical example of Nazi training. On some unused land next to our Camp, a *Hitlerjugend*—Hitler Youth—encampment had been set up. There were possibly two hundred adolescents, still almost children. In the mornings they practiced flag-raising, sang belligerent hymns, and, armed with ancient muskets, were put through marching and shooting drills. We understood later that they were being prepared for enrollment in the Volkssturm, that ragtag army of old men and children that, according to the Führer's mad plans, was supposed to put up a last-ditch defense against the advancing Russians. But sometimes in the afternoon their instructors, who were SS veterans, would bring them to see us as we worked clearing away rubble from the bombings, or erecting slapdash and useless little protective walls of bricks or sandbags.

They led them among us on a "guided tour" and lectured them in loud voices, as if we had neither ears to hear nor the intelligence to understand. "These that you see are the enemies of the Reich, *your* enemies. Take a good look at them: would you call them men? They are *Untermenschen*, submen! They stink because they don't wash; they're in rags because they don't take care of

88   themselves. What's more, many of them don't even understand German. They are subversives, bandits, street thieves from the four corners of Europe, but we have rendered them harmless; now they work for us, but they are good only for the most primitive work. Moreover, it is only right that they should repair the war damages; these are the people who wanted the war: the Jews, the Communists, and the agents of the plutocracies."

The child-soldiers listened, devout and dazed. Seen close up, they inspired both pain and horror. They were haggard and frightened, yet they looked at us with intense hatred. So we were the ones guilty for all the evils, the cities in ruins, the famine, their dead fathers on the Russian front. The Führer was stern but just, and it was just to serve him.

At that time I worked as a "specialist" in a chemical laboratory inside the plant: these are things that I have written about elsewhere, but, strangely, with the passing of the years these memories do not fade, nor do they thin out. They become enriched with details I thought were forgotten, which sometimes acquire meaning in the light of other people's memories, from letters I receive or books I read.

It was snowing, it was very cold, and working in that laboratory was not easy. At times the heating system didn't work and at night ice would form, bursting the phials of reagents and the big bottle of distilled water. Often we lacked the raw materials or reagents necessary for analyses, and it was necessary to improvise or to produce what was missing on the spot. There was no ethyl acetate for a colorimetric measurement. The laboratory head told me to prepare a liter of it and gave me the needed acetic acid and ethyl alcohol. It's a simple procedure; I had done it in Turin in my organic preparations course in 1941. Only three years before, but it seemed like three thousand. . . . Everything went smoothly up to the final distillation, but at that point suddenly the water stopped running.

This could have ended in a small disaster, because I was using a glass refrigerator. If the water returned, the refrigerating tube, which had been heated on the inside by the product's vapor, would certainly have shattered on contact with the icy water. I turned off the faucet, found a small pail, filled it with distilled water, and immersed in it the small pump of a Höppler thermostat. The pump pushed the water into the refrigerator, and the hot water fell into the pail as it came out. Everything went well for a few minutes, then I noticed that the ethyl acetate was no longer condensing; almost all of it was coming out of the pipe in the form of vapor. I had been able to find only a small amount of distilled water (there was no other) and by now it had become warm.

What to do? There was a lot of snow on the windowsills, so I made balls with it and put them into the pail one by one. While I was busy with my gray snowballs, Dr. Pannwitz, the German chemist who had subjected me to a singular "state examination" to determine whether my professional knowledge was sufficient, came into the lab. He was a fanatical Nazi. He looked suspiciously at my makeshift installation and the murky water that could have damaged the precious pump, but said nothing and left.

A few days later, toward the middle of December, the basin of one of the suction hoods was blocked and the chief told me to unplug it. It seemed natural to him that the dirty job should fall to me and not to the lab technician, a girl named Frau Mayer, and actually it seemed natural to me too. I was the only one who could stretch out serenely on the floor without fear of getting dirty; my striped suit was already completely filthy. . . .

I was getting up after having screwed the siphon back on when I noticed Frau Mayer standing close to me. She spoke to me in a whisper with a guilty air; she was the only one of the eight or ten girls in the lab—German, Polish, and Ukrainian—who showed no contempt for me. Since my hands were already dirty, she asked, could I fix her bicycle, which had a flat? She would, of course, give me something for my trouble.

This apparently neutral request was actually full of sociological implications. She had said "please" to me, which in itself represented an infraction of the upside-down code that regulated our relationships with the Germans. She had spoken to me for reasons not connected with work; she had made a kind of contract with me, and a contract is made between equals; and she had expressed, or at least implied, gratitude for the work I had done on the basin in her stead. However, the girl was also inviting me to break the rules, which could be very dangerous for me, since I was there as a chemist, and by

repairing her bike I would be taking time away from my
professional work. She was proposing, in other words, a
kind of complicity, risky but potentially useful. Having
a human relationship with someone "on the other side"
involved danger, a social promotion, and more food for
today and the day after. In a flash I did the algebraic sum
of the three addends: hunger won by several lengths, and
I accepted the proposal.

Frau Mayer held out the key to the padlock, saying
that I should go and get the bicycle; it was in the court-
yard. That was out of the question; I explained as best I
could that she must go herself, or send someone else.
"We" were by definition thieves and liars: if anybody
saw me with a bicycle I'd really be in for it. Another problem arose when I saw the bicycle. In its tool bag there
were pieces of rubber, rubber cement, and small irons to
remove the tire, but there was no pump, and without a
pump I couldn't locate the hole in the inner tube. I must
explain, incidentally, that in those days bicycles and flat
tires were much more common than they are now, and
almost all Europeans, especially young ones, knew how
to patch a tire. A pump? No problem, said Frau Mayer;
all I had to do was get Meister Grubach, her colleague
next door, to lend me one. But this too wasn't so simple.
With some embarrassment I had to ask her to write and
sign a note: "*Bitte um die Fahrradpumpe.*"

I made the repair, and Frau Mayer, in great secrecy,
gave me a hardboiled egg and four lumps of sugar. Don't
misunderstand; given the situation and the going rates, it
was a more than generous reward. As she furtively slipped

me the packet, she whispered something that gave me a lot to think about: "Christmas will soon be here." Obvious words, absurd actually when addressed to a Jewish prisoner; certainly they were intended to mean something else, something no German at that time would have dared to put into words.

In telling this story after forty years, I'm not trying to make excuses for Nazi Germany. One human German does not whitewash the innumerable inhuman or indifferent ones, but it does have the merit of breaking a stereotype.

It was a memorable Christmas for the world at war; memorable for me too, because it was marked by a miracle. At Auschwitz, the various categories of prisoners (political, common criminals, social misfits, homosexuals, etc.) were allowed to receive gift packages from home, but not the Jews. Anyway, from whom could the Jews have received them? From their families, exterminated or confined in the surviving ghettos? From the very few who had escaped the roundups, hidden in cellars, in attics, terrified and penniless? And who knew our address? For all the world knew, we were dead.

And yet a package did finally find its way to me, through a chain of friends, sent by my sister and my mother, who were hidden in Italy. The last link of that chain was Lorenzo Perrone, the bricklayer from Fossano, of whom I have spoken in *Survival in Auschwitz*, and whose heartbreaking end I have recounted here in "Lorenzo's Return." The package contained ersatz chocolate, cookies, and powdered milk, but to describe its real value, the impact it had on me and on my friend Alberto, is beyond the powers of ordinary language. In the Camp, the terms eating, food, hunger, had meanings totally different from their usual ones. That unexpected, improbable, impossible package was like a meteorite, a heavenly object, charged with symbols, immensely precious, and with an enormous momentum.

We were no longer alone: a link with the outside world had been established, and there were delicious things to eat for days and days. But there were also serious practical problems to resolve immediately: we found ourselves in the situation of a passerby who is handed a gold ingot in full view of everyone. Where to put the food? How to keep it? How to protect it from other people's greediness? How to invest it wisely? Our year-old hunger kept pushing us toward the worst possible solution: to eat everything right then and there. But we had to resist that temptation. Our weakened stomachs could not have coped with the abuse; within an hour, it would have ended in indigestion or worse.

We had no safe hiding places so we distributed the food in all the regular pockets in our clothes, and sewed secret ones inside the backs of our jackets so that even in case of a body search something could be saved. But to have to take everything with us, to work, to the wash-house, to the latrine, was inconvenient and awkward. Alberto and I talked it over at length in the evening, after curfew. The two of us had made a pact: everything either one of us managed to scrounge beyond our ration

94 had to be divided into two exactly equal parts. Alberto was always more successful than I in these enterprises, and I often asked why he wanted to stay partners with anyone as inefficient as I was. But he always replied: "You never know. I'm faster but you're luckier." For once, he turned out to be right.

Alberto came up with an ingenious scheme. The cookies were the biggest problem. We had them stored, a few here, a few there. I even had some in the lining of my cap, and had to be careful not to crush them when I had to yank it off fast to salute a passing SS. The cookies weren't all that good but they looked nice. We could, he suggested, divide them into two packages and give them as gifts to the Kapo and the barracks Elder. According to Alberto, that was the best investment. We would acquire prestige, and the two big shots, even without a formal agreement, would reward us with various favors. The rest of the food we could eat ourselves, in small, reasonable daily rations, and with the greatest possible precautions.

But in Camp, the crowding, the total lack of privacy, the gossip and disorder were such that our secret quickly became an open one. In the space of a few days we noticed that our companions and Kapos were looking at us with different eyes. That's the point: they were looking at us the way you do at something or someone outside the norm, that no longer melts into the background but stands out. According to how much they liked "the two Italians," they looked at us with envy, with understanding, complacency, or open desire. Mendi, a Slovakian rabbi friend of mine, winked at me and said "*Mazel tov*," the lovely Yiddish and Hebrew phrase used to congratulate someone on a happy event. Quite a few people knew or had guessed something, which made us both happy and uneasy; we would have to be on our guard. In any case, we decided by mutual consent to speed up the consumption: something eaten cannot be stolen.

On Christmas Day we worked as usual. As a matter of fact, since the laboratory was closed, I was sent along with the others to remove rubble and carry sacks of chemical products from a bombed warehouse to an undamaged one. When I got back to Camp in the evening, I went to the washhouse. I still had quite a lot of chocolate and powdered milk in my pockets, so I waited until there was a free spot in the corner farthest from the entrance. I hung my jacket on a nail, right behind me; no one could have approached without my seeing him. I began to wash, when out of the corner of my eye I saw my jacket rising in the air. I turned but it was already too late. The jacket, with all its contents, and with my registration number sewed on the breast, was already out of reach. Someone had lowered a string and hook from the small window above the nail. I ran outside, half undressed as I was, but no one was there. No one had seen anything, no one knew anything. Along with everything else, I was now without a jacket. I had to go to the barracks supplymaster to confess my "crime," because in the Camp being robbed was a crime. He gave me another jacket, but ordered me to find a needle and thread, never

96 mind how, rip the registration number off my pants and sew it on the new jacket as quickly as possible. Otherwise *"bekommst du fünfundzwanzig"*: I'd get twenty-five whacks with a stick.

We divided up the contents of Alberto's pockets. His had remained unscathed, and he proceeded to display his finest philosophical resources. We two had eaten more than half of the food, right? And the rest wasn't completely wasted. Some other famished man was celebrating Christmas at our expense, maybe even blessing us. And anyway, we could be sure of one thing: that this would be our last Christmas of war and imprisonment.

The Quiet City

I T MIGHT BE surprising that in the Camps one of the most frequent states of mind was curiosity. And yet, besides being frightened, humiliated, and desperate, we were curious: hungry for bread and also to understand. The world around us was upside down and so somebody must have turned it upside down, and for that reason he himself must have been upside down: one, a thousand, a million antihuman beings created to twist that which was straight, to befoul that which was clean. It was an unpermissible simplification, but at that time and in that place we were not capable of complex ideas.

As regards the lords of evil, this curiosity, which is not limited to the Nazi chiefs, still lingers. Hundreds of books have come out on the psychology of Hitler, Stalin, Himmler, Goebbels, and I have read dozens of them and been left unsatisfied: but probably it is a matter here of the essential inadequacy of documentary evidence. It al-

100 most never has the power to give us the depths of a human being; for this purpose the dramatist or poet are more appropriate than the historian or psychologist.

Nevertheless, this search of mine has not been entirely fruitless: a strange, indeed provocative fate some years ago put me on the track of "someone on the other side," not certainly one of the greats of evil, perhaps not even a fully qualified villain, but nevertheless a specimen and a witness. A witness in spite of himself, who did not want to be one, but who has testified without wanting to, and perhaps even unknowingly. Those who bear witness by their behavior are the most valuable witnesses, because they are certainly truthful.

He was an almost-me, another myself, turned upside down. We were contemporaries, not dissimilar in education, perhaps not even in character. He, Mertens, was a young chemist, German and Catholic, and I a young chemist, Italian and Jewish. Potentially two colleagues: in fact we worked in the same factory, but I was inside the barbed wire and he outside. However, there were forty thousand of us employed in the Buna Works at Auschwitz. That the two of us, he an *Oberingenieur* and I a slave-chemist, ever met is improbable, and in any case no longer verifiable, nor did we ever see each other later on.

Whatever I know about him comes from letters of mutual friends. The world turns out to be laughably small at times, small enough to permit two chemists from different countries to find themselves linked by a chain of acquaintances who help to weave a network of exchanged information, which is a poor substitute for a direct encounter but still better than mutual ignorance. By such means I learned that Mertens had read my books about the Camp and, in all likelihood, others as well, because he was neither cynical nor insensitive. He tended to block out a certain segment of his past, but was intelligent enough to keep from lying to himself. He did not make himself a gift of lies, but blanks, lacunae.

The first report I have of him goes back to the end of 1941, a period of rethinking for all Germans still capable of reasoning and resisting propaganda. The victorious Japanese are overrunning all of Southeast Asia, the Germans are laying siege to Leningrad and are at the doors of Moscow, but the era of the blitzes is over, the collapse of Russia has not taken place. Instead, aerial bombings of the German cities have begun. Now the war involves everybody. In every family there is at least one man at the front, and no man at the front is sure any longer of the safety of his family: behind the house doors, warmongering rhetoric no longer carries much weight.

Mertens is a chemist in a metropolitan rubber factory, and the manager of the firm makes him a proposal that is almost an order: he will find career, and perhaps also political, advantages if he accepts an offer to transfer to the Buna Works at Auschwitz. It's a tranquil zone, far removed from the front and outside the range of the bombers. The work is the same, the salary better, and there will be no difficulty about housing: many Polish houses are empty. . . . Mertens talks it over with his

102 colleagues. Most of them advise against it; one doesn't exchange the certain for the uncertain, and besides, the Buna Works are in an ugly, marshy, and unhealthy region. Unhealthy even historically, Upper Silesia is one of those corners of Europe that have changed masters too many times and are inhabited by mixed peoples, hostile to one another.

But no one has objections to the name Auschwitz: it is still an empty name that does not provoke echoes; one of the many Polish towns which have changed their names since the German occupation. Oswiecim has become Auschwitz, as if that is enough to change into German the Poles who have lived there for centuries. It is a small town like many others.

Mertens thinks about it; he is engaged and to set up a household in Germany, under the bombings, would be foolhardy. He asks for a short leave and goes to have a look. What he thought during this first survey is not known: the man went back, got married, spoke to no one, and left again for Auschwitz with wife and furniture to settle down there. His friends, those in fact who wrote the story for me, asked him to speak but he remains silent.

Nor did he speak the second time he was seen in Germany, in the summer of 1943, on vacation (because even in wartime in Nazi Germany, people went on vacation in August). Now the scenario has changed: Italian fascism, defeated on all fronts, has come apart and the Allies are pushing up the peninsula. The aerial battle against the British is lost and by now no corner of Germany is spared from pitiless Allied retaliation. Not only did the Russians not collapse but at Stalingrad they inflicted on the Germans and on Hitler himself, who directed the operations with the obstinacy of a madman, the most scathing defeat.

The Mertens couple are the objects of very guarded curiosity, because at this point despite all precautions Auschwitz is no longer an empty name. There have been rumors, imprecise but sinister: it must be put alongside Dachau and Buchenwald. It seems that it may even be worse. It is one of those places about which it is risky to ask questions, but after all, we're all intimate friends here, from way back; Mertens has come from the place; he surely must know something, and if he does he should say so.

But, while all the living-room conversations interweave, the women talking about evacuations and black market, the men about their work, and someone in a whisper tells the latest anti-Nazi joke, Mertens goes off by himself. In the next room there is a piano; he plays and drinks, returns to the living room now and again, only to pour himself another glass. By midnight he is drunk but his host has not lost sight of him; he drags him to the table and says to him loud and clear, "Now you're going to sit down here and tell us what the hell is happening down there, and why you have to get drunk instead of talking to us."

Mertens feels torn between intoxication, caution, and a certain need to confess. "Auschwitz is a Camp," he says, "actually a group of Camps; one is right next to the

104 plant. There are men and women, filthy, ragged, they
don't speak German. And they do the most exhausting
work. We are not allowed to talk to them."

"Who says you can't?"

"Management. When we arrived we were told that
they are dangerous, bandits and subversives."

"And you have never talked to them?" asks the host.

"No," Mertens replies, pouring himself another
drink.

Here young Mrs. Mertens joins in: "I met a woman
who cleaned the manager's house. All she said to me was
'Frau, Brot' . . . Lady, bread . . . but I . . ."

Mertens mustn't have been all that drunk after all
because he says brusquely to his wife: "Stop it!" and,
turning to the others: "Would you mind changing the
subject?"

I don't know much about Mertens's behavior after
the collapse of Germany. I do know that he and his wife,
like many other Germans of the eastern regions, fled before the Soviets down the interminable roads of defeat,
covered with snow, rubble, and corpses, and that afterwards he went back to his profession of technician, but
refusing all contacts and withdrawing more and more
into himself.

He spoke a little more, many years after the end of
the war, when there was no more Gestapo to frighten
him. This time he was questioned by a "specialist," an ex-
prisoner who today is a famous historian of the Camps,
Hermann Langbein. In reply to precise questions, he
said he had agreed to move to Auschwitz to prevent a

Nazi from going in his place, that for fear of punishment
he had never spoken to the prisoners, but had always
tried to alleviate their working conditions; that at that
time he knew nothing about the gas chambers because
he had not asked anyone about anything. Didn't he realize that his obedience was a concrete help to the Hitler
regime? Yes, today he did, but not at the time. It had
never entered his mind.

I never tried to meet Mertens. I felt a complex re-
luctance, of which aversion was only one component.
Years ago I wrote him a letter; I told him that if Hitler
had risen to power, devastated Europe and brought Germany to ruin, it was because many good German citizens
behaved the way he did, trying not to see and keeping
silent about what they did see. Mertens never answered
me, and he died a few years later.

Small Causes

A FEW DAYS AGO in a group of friends we were talking about the influence of small causes on the course of history. This is a classic controversy, classically lacking a definitive and absolute solution: it can be safely affirmed that the history of the world (well, let's be more modest and say the history of the Mediterranean basin) would have been completely different if Cleopatra's nose had been longer, as Pascal would have it, and just as safely you can affirm that it would have been exactly the same, as Marxist orthodoxy and the historiography proposed by Tolstoy in *War and Peace* contend. Since it is not possible to conjure up a Cleopatra with a different nose but surrounded by exactly the same world as the historical Cleopatra's, there is no possibility of proving or disproving either thesis; the problem is a pseudoproblem. Real problems sooner or later are resolved; on the contrary, pseudoproblems are not. So, not being open

110 to definitive solution, they are extremely long-lived: the one under discussion is many centuries old, and destined to live that long again.

We all agreed, at any rate, with the observation that small causes can have a determining effect on individual histories, just as moving the pointer of a railroad switch by a few inches can shunt a train with one thousand passengers aboard to Madrid instead of Hamburg. A pistol bullet that severs a carotid artery has a very different effect from one that only grazes it. And a casual encounter, a bet at roulette, a lightning bolt . . .

At this moment, everyone present insisted on telling about the small cause that had radically changed his life, and I too, when the excitement had abated, told mine, or, to be more precise, I refined the details, since I had already told the story many times, both in conversation and in writing.

Forty years ago I was a prisoner in Auschwitz, working in a chemical laboratory. I was hungry and on the lookout for something small and unusual (and therefore of high commercial value) to steal and exchange for bread. After various attempts (some successful, some not), I found a drawer full of pipettes. Pipettes are small glass tubes, precisely graduated, which are used to transfer exact amounts of liquid from one container to another. Nowadays more hygienic methods are employed, but at the time this was done by sucking up the liquid so that it rose exactly to the desired marking, then letting it descend by its own weight. There were a lot of pipettes. I slipped a dozen into a hidden pocket I had

sewed inside my jacket, and took them back to the 111
Camp. They are graceful, delicate objects, and on the
way back several of them broke. Anyway, as soon as roll
call was over and before the distribution of the evening
soup began, I ran to the infirmary and offered the un-
broken ones to a Polish male nurse whom I knew and
who worked in the Contagious Ward, explaining that
they could be used for clinical analyses.

The Pole looked at my booty with little interest and
then told me that for that day it was too late; he no
longer had any bread. All he could offer me was a bit of
soup. He was a shrewd bargainer and knew that I had no
choice. To carry those obviously stolen goods around in
the Camp was dangerous, and there was nobody else I
could offer them to. He enjoyed a monopoly and took
advantage of it.

I accepted the proposed payment; the Pole disappeared among the patients of his ward and came back
shortly with a bowl half full of soup, but half full in a
curious way: vertically. It was very cold, the soup had
frozen, and someone had removed half of it with a spoon,
like someone eating half a cake. Who could have left
half a bowl of soup in that reign of hunger? Almost certainly someone who had died halfway through the meal,
and, given the sort of place this was, someone sick with
a contagious disease. In the last weeks, diphtheria and
scarlet fever had broken out in the Camp in epidemic
proportions.

But at Auschwitz we didn't observe precautions of
this kind. First came hunger, then all the rest; leaving

112 something edible uneaten was not what is commonly called "a shame," it was unthinkable, indeed physically impossible. That same evening, my alter ego, Alberto, and I shared the suspect soup. Alberto was my age, had the same build, temperament, and profession as I, and we slept in the same bunk. We even looked somewhat alike; the foreign comrades and the Kapo considered it superfluous to distinguish between us. They constantly confused us, and demanded that whether they called "Alberto" or "Primo," whichever one of us happened to be closest should answer.

We were interchangeable, so to speak, and anyone would have predicted for us two the same fate: we would both go under or both survive. But it was just at this point that the switch-pointer came into play, the small cause with the determining effects: Alberto had had scarlet fever as a child and was immune; I was not.

I realized the consequences of our rashness a few days later. At reveille, while Alberto felt perfectly all right, I had a bad sore throat, I had trouble swallowing and had a high fever, but "reporting" sick in the morning was not allowed, so I went to the lab as I did every day. I felt deathly sick but on that day of all days I was given an unusual task. In that lab, half a dozen girls, German, Polish, and Ukrainian, worked, or pretended to work. The head of the lab called me aside and told me I must teach Fräulein Drechsel an analytical method which I myself had learned only a few weeks before. Fräulein Drechsel was a chubby German adolescent, clumsy, sullen, and dumb. Most of the time she avoided looking at us three slave-chemists. When she did, her dull eyes expressed a vague hostility, made up of mistrust, embarrassment, revulsion, and fear. She had never addressed a word to me. I found her disagreeable and distrusted her as well, because on preceding days I had seen her slink off with the very young SS man who watched over that department. And besides, she alone wore a swastika badge pinned to her shirt. She might have been a Hitler Youth squadron-leader.

She was a very bad pupil because of her stupidity, and I was a very bad teacher because I didn't feel well, didn't speak German well, and above all because I wasn't motivated; if anything, I was countermotivated. Why in the world should I have to teach that creature anything? The normal teacher-pupil relationship, which is a descending one, came into conflict with ascending relationships: I was Jewish and she was Aryan, I was dirty and sick, she was clean and healthy.

I believe it was the only time I have deliberately done someone wrong. The analytical method I was supposed to teach her involved the use of a pipette: a sister of those to which I owed the illness coursing through my veins. I took one from the drawer and showed Fräulein Drechsel how to use it, inserting it between my feverish lips, then held it out to her and invited her to do the same. In short, I did all I could to infect her.

A few days later, while I was in the infirmary, the Camp broke up under the tragic circumstances that have been described many times. Alberto was a victim of the small cause, of the scarlet fever from which he had re-

114 covered as a child. He came to say goodbye, then went into the night and the snow together with sixty thousand other unfortunates, on that deadly march from which few returned alive. I was saved in the most unpredictable way by that business of the stolen pipettes, which gave me a providential sickness exactly at the moment when, paradoxically, not being able to walk was a godsend. In fact, for reasons never clarified, at Auschwitz the fleeing Nazis abstained from carrying out explicit orders from Berlin: Leave no witnesses behind. They left the Camp in a hurry, and abandoned us who were sick to our fate.

As for Fräulein Drechsel, I know nothing about what happened to her. Since it may be that she was guilty of nothing more than a few Nazi kisses, I hope that my deed, the small cause set in motion by me, did not bring her grievous harm. At seventeen scarlet fever is cured quickly and leaves no serious aftereffects. In any case, I feel no remorse for my private attempt at bacteriological warfare. Later on, reading books on the subject, I learned that other people in other Camps had taken better-aimed and more systematic action. In places ravaged by exanthematic typhus—often fatal, and transmitted by lice in clothing—the prisoners who washed and ironed the SS uniforms would search for comrades who had died of typhus, pick lice off the corpses, and slip them under the collars of the ironed and spruced-up military jackets. Lice are not very attractive animals, but they do not have racial prejudices.

The Story of Avrom

I<small>T OFTEN HAPPENS</small> these days that you hear people say they're ashamed of being Italian. In fact we have good reasons to be ashamed: first and foremost, of not having been able to produce a political class that represents us and, on the contrary, tolerating for thirty years one that does not. On the other hand, we have virtues of which we are unaware, and we do not realize how rare they are in Europe and in the world. I recall these virtues every time I happen to repeat the story of Avrom (I will give him that name), a story I came to know by chance. For now, the story lives in just this way, like a saga transmitted from mouth to mouth, with the risk that it will become distorted or embellished and that it may be mistaken for a fictional invention. It is a story I like because it contains an image of our country seen by naive and foreign eyes, in an unwavering light of salvation, and what's more, seen in its most beautiful hour. I will sum it up here, apologizing for possible inexactness.

118   In 1939 Avrom was thirteen. He was a Polish Jew, son of a very poor hatmaker from Lvov. When the Germans entered Poland, Avrom quickly understood that it was better not to wait for them shut up in the house. That is what his parents had decided to do and they were promptly captured and killed. Left alone, Avrom hid out in the depths of the small local criminal underworld and lived by small thefts, small-scale smuggling, the black market, vague and precarious pursuits, sleeping in the cellars of bombed-out houses until he learned that in his town there was a barracks of Italians. It was probably one of the bases of ARMIR.* In the city people quickly spread the story that the Italian soldiers were different from the Germans—they were good-hearted, took out the local girls, and weren't all that fussy about military discipline, permits, and prohibitions. By the end of 1942 Avrom had taken up permanent and semiofficial residence in the barracks. He had learned a little Italian and tried to make himself useful by doing a variety of odd jobs: interpreter, shoeshine boy, messenger. He had become the barracks mascot but he was not the only one. About a dozen other boys and small children who had been abandoned, who had no parents or homes or means, lived there like him. They were Jews and Christians; for the Italians this seemed to make no difference whatsoever, and Avrom never ceased being amazed by it.

In January 1943 ARMIR was routed, and the barracks filled with stragglers; then ARMIR was demobi-

* ARMIR: *Armata Italiana in Russia*

lized. All the Italians were returning to Italy, and the officials let it be understood that if anyone wanted to take along those parentless kids, they would look the other way. Avrom had become friends with an Alpine soldier from the Canavese. They crossed the Tarvisio on the same troop train and the Fascist government confined them in the same quarantine camp at Mestre. It was called a sanitary quarantine, and after all they did have lice, but actually it was a political quarantine, because Mussolini didn't want those veterans to talk too much about what they had seen. They stayed there until September 12th, when the Germans arrived, as though they were pursuing Avrom personally, driving him out of every hiding place in Europe. The Germans sealed off the camp and loaded everybody on freight trains to transport them to Germany.

In the freight car Avrom told his Alpine friend that he was not going to Germany because he knew all about the Germans and what they were capable of: better to throw yourself off the train. The Alpino replied that he too had seen what the Germans had done in Russia, but that he did not have the courage to jump. He said that if Avrom jumped, however, he would give him a letter for his parents in the Canavese, saying that the boy was a friend of his, that they should give him his own bed and treat him just as if it were he. Avrom did jump off the train, with the letter in his pocket. He was in Italy, but not in the glossy, gleaming Italy of the picture postcards and geography textbooks. He was alone, on the railbed, penniless, in the middle of the night, surrounded by

120 German patrols in an unknown country somewhere between Venice and the Brenner Pass. All he knew was that he had to reach the Canavese. Everyone helped him, and no one gave him away. He found a train that was going to Milan, then one for Turin. At Porta Susa Station he took the local train, got off at Cuorgnè, and set out on foot for his friend's small village. At that point he was seventeen.

The Alpino's parents gave him a nice welcome, but didn't say much. They gave him clothes, food, and a bed, and, since two young arms came in handy, they put him to work in the fields. In those months Italy was full of displaced people, among whom there were also English, Americans, Australians, Russians, who had escaped on September 8th from prisoner-of-war camps. So no one paid much attention to the foreign boy. No one asked him questions except the parish priest who, after talking to him, realized he was quick-witted and told the Alpino's parents it was a shame not to send him to school. So they sent him to the priests' school. Avrom, who had been through a lot, enjoyed going to school and studying. It gave him a feeling of tranquillity and normalcy. However, he found it amusing that they made him study Latin. Why should Italian boys need to learn Latin when Italian was almost the same thing? But he studied everything diligently, got very good grades in all his subjects, and in March the priest called him up to serve Mass. This business of a Jewish boy serving Mass struck him as even funnier, but he still did not tell anyone that he was Jewish, because one never knows. In any case he soon learned to make the sign of the cross and learned all the Christian prayers.

Early in April, a truck full of Germans suddenly showed up in the village square and everyone fled. Then they noticed that these were strange Germans: they didn't bark out commands or threats, didn't, in fact, speak German but rather a language the villagers had never heard before, and tried politely to make themselves understood. Someone had the idea of looking for Avrom, who was himself a foreigner. Avrom arrived in the square and he and those "Germans" understood each other very well because they weren't Germans at all: they were Czechs who had been conscripted into the Wehrmacht, and now they had deserted, appropriating a military truck, and they wanted to join the Italian partisans. They spoke Czech, and Avrom answered in Polish, but they understood each other all the same. Avrom thanked his Canavese friends and went off with the Czechs. He did not have well-defined political views but he had seen what the Germans did to his country, and it seemed right to fight against them.

The Czechs joined a division of Italian partisans who operated in the Orco valley, and Avrom stayed with them as interpreter and courier. One of the Italian partisans was Jewish and told everyone so. This astonished Avrom, but he continued to keep quiet about also being Jewish. There was a German mop-up and his detachment had to go up the valley all the way to Ceresole Reale, where he was told that it was called Reale (royal) because the King of Italy used to come there to hunt

122 chamois. They showed him through binoculars the chamois on the slopes of Gran Paradiso. Avrom was dazzled by the beauty of the mountains, lake, and woods, and it seemed absurd to him to come there to fight a war. There was a skirmish with the Fascists who came up from Locana, then the partisans retreated into the valleys of Lanzo across the Colle della Crocetta. For the boy, who came from the ghetto horror and a flat, gray Poland, that crossing through the rugged, deserted mountain, and the many others that followed, were the revelation of a splendid new world of experiences that intoxicated and overwhelmed him: the beauty of creation, freedom, and trust in his companions. More combat and other marches ensued and in the autumn of 1944 his group descended the Val Susa, from village to village, as far as Sant'Ambrogio.

By this time Avrom was a seasoned partisan, courageous and strong; deeply disciplined by nature, he was adept with pistol and machine gun, polyglot, and wily as a fox. An agent of the American Secret Service heard about him and entrusted Avrom with a radio transmitter. It fitted into a suitcase which he had to carry with him, shifting it continually so it would not be detected by the radio direction-finder. He was to maintain radio contact with the armies that were moving up Italy from the south, and most especially with Anders's Poles. Shifting from hiding place to hiding place, Avrom arrived in Turin. He had been given the address of a parish church in the center of the city, and the password. April 25th found him holed up with his radio in a tiny room in the 123 belfry.

After the Liberation the Allies summoned him to Rome in order to regularize his position, which was actually rather confused. They loaded him on a jeep and, through the bombed streets, through towns and villages crowded with ragged people who were applauding, he reached Liguria. And for the first time in his young life, he saw the sea.

The story of the exploits of eighteen-year-old Avrom, innocent soldier of fortune, who, like so many Nordic travelers of old, had discovered Italy with a virgin eye, and, like so many heroes of the Risorgimento, had fought for the freedom of everyone in a country that was not his, ends here, before the splendor of a peaceful Mediterranean.

Now Avrom lives in a kibbutz in Israel. He, a polyglot, no longer has a language that is truly his. He has almost forgotten his Polish, Czech, and Italian, and has not yet acquired full mastery of Hebrew. In this language, which is new to him, he has set down his memories in the form of bare and unpretentious notes, veiled by the distance of time and space. He is a modest person, and he has recorded them without the ambitions of the literary man or historian, and with his children and grandchildren in mind, so that a record of the things he saw and lived will be preserved. It is to be hoped that they will find someone who will restore them to the full breath of life that is inherently in them.

Tired of Imposture

ANYONE WHO HAS the opportunity to compare the true image of a writer with what can be deduced from his writings knows how frequently they do not coincide. The delicate investigator of movements of the spirit, vibrant as an oscillating circuit, proves to be a pompous oaf, morbidly full of himself, greedy for money and adulation, blind to his neighbor's suffering. The orgiastic and sumptuous poet, in Dionysiac communion with the universe, is an abstinent, abstemious little man, not by ascetic choice but by medical prescription.

But how pleasant and cheering is the opposite case: the man who remains true to himself in what he writes; even if he is not brilliant our sympathy goes immediately out to him. Here there no longer are deceit or transfiguration, Muses or quantum leaps. The mask is the face, and the reader seems to be looking from a height at a clear body of water and distinguishing the multicolored peb-

128 bles on the bottom. I had this feeling several years ago when reading the German manuscript of an autobiography that came out subsequently in Italian in 1973, and later in English, entitled *Escape from the Nazi Dragnets*. The author's name was Joel König, and not by chance the first chapter is entitled "Tired of Imposture." König is not a professional writer; he is a biologist and has picked up his pen only because he thought that his story was too unusual not to be recorded.

Joel, a German Jew, born in 1922 in Heilbronn in Swabia, writes with the candor and shortcomings of the nonprofessional; he often dwells too long on the superfluous and neglects essential facts. He is a middle-class boy, son of a provincial rabbi, and since childhood he has observed the complex Jewish ritual without any feeling of constraint, rebellion, or irony, indeed, feeling he was reliving an ancient tradition that is joyful and imbued with symbolic poetry.

His father has taught him that true enough every person has received from God only one soul, but on the Sabbath God grants the loan of another to every pious man, which illuminates and sanctifies him from sunset to sunset. Therefore, not only doesn't one work on the Sabbath, but one mustn't even touch tools such as a hammer, scissors, pen, and money least of all, so as not to corrupt the Sabbath soul. Children may not even catch butterflies, because to do so comes under the concept of hunting, which in turn comes under the larger concept of labor. Moreover, the Sabbath is the day of freedom for everyone, even for the animals. Besides, ani-

mals too honor the Creator. When they drink, chickens 129
lift their beaks to heaven to thank Him for each single
sip.

In 1933 Hitler's black shadow begins to spread over
this "Swabian idyll." In the meantime, the father has
been transferred (still as a rabbi) to a small town in
Upper Silesia, not far from Auschwitz, but the Auschwitz of those days is an ordinary small border town.
Joel and his father react to the new climate in a way that
is very instructive inasmuch as it teaches us essential
facts about the Germany of then and today.

The rabbi has taught his son that the Treaty of Ver-
sailles, after the original sin and the destruction of the
Temple at the hands of Titus, was the most calamitous
event in world history, but that, nevertheless, German
Jews must not meet injustice with violence. "To suffer
unjustly is better than to act unjustly." During the years
of economic crisis he voted for the Catholics of the Center "because they fear God," but in '33 the Catholics
vote full powers to Hitler, and in the Nuremberg Laws
he sees God's warning hand, and punishment for the
transgressions of the Jews. Did they do business on the
Sabbath? Now their stores are being boycotted. Did they
marry Christian women? The new providential laws pro-
hibit mixed marriages.

The Nazi nets tighten around the German Jews:
only a few farsighted ones try to flee to neutral countries,
or seek precarious refuge in a clandestine existence; the
larger part, like Joel's parents, live from day to day,
dazed, feeding on absurd illusions and false information,

130 while every day, with refined cruelty that progresses inexorably, law after law is passed with the deliberate intent of inflicting humiliation and suffering.

In an impious parody of ritual norms, instead of the words of the Lord next to their hearts and on the doorposts of their houses, the Jews must wear the yellow star; they are not allowed to own bicycles or telephones, cannot use public phones, or subscribe to newspapers. They must hand over woolen clothes and furs, and their food rations are at famine level; transfers "to the east" begin in a trickle; people are thinking of ghettos, forced labor. Nobody suspects the slaughter and yet even the dying and children are being deported . . .

Like many other young people, Joel takes refuge in a farm-school organized by the Zionists, its purpose to train boys and girls for agricultural work and communal living, with an eye to an ever less likely emigration to Palestine. The Gestapo tolerates this because labor is very scarce and the enterprise is profitable (the young people are not paid). But little by little the farm turns into a miniature Camp; Joel rips off his yellow star and escapes to Berlin.

Shortly thereafter his parents are deported and Joel is left alone in the hostile city, which is ravaged and convulsed by bombings and is swarming with spies, police, and foreign workers of all races. He has destroyed his documents, countersigned with the letter J, for Jew, and has no ration cards; he is an outlaw. Well, it would seem that just in this situation of extreme alienation this young man, in love with celestial and terrestrial order, discovers

himself and becomes aware of his own extraordinary resources.

He becomes a Chaplinesque hero, at once naive and
shrewd, open to imaginative improvisation, never desperate, fundamentally incapable of hatred or violence, in
love with life, adventure, and joy. He gets past every trap
and ambush as if by a miracle: as if God's pact with the
people of Israel has found in him and for him practical
application; as if God Himself, in whom he believes, held
a hand over his head as it is believed He does with children and drunks.

He finds a first precarious refuge with an old shoemaker, who agrees to take him in, not so much out of
generosity but from foolishness. He does not realize that
giving shelter to a Jew in the Berlin of the Gestapo can
cost one's life, but Joel knows, and in order not to com-
promise an innocent he once again takes off. Where to
spend the nights in the harsh winter of '42–'43? In the
operating cab of a crane, in the sheds for fire-fighting
equipment, in the carcass of a Soviet tank displayed in
the square like a monument? Joel chooses at random and
it always goes well.

He roams around Berlin, a desert of rubble separated from the sky by immense camouflage nets, and
temporarily settles in an abandoned latrine; two cubic
yards but it's better than nothing. Fond of cleanliness,
he diligently inspects the buildings gutted by bombs and
finds water-heaters that are still functioning, even if the
fourth wall is missing: taking due precautions, possibly
with the help of an accomplice, one can even take a hot

132 bath. It is a delight, and besides, the oddity of the invention affords Joel a keen childish amusement that lends spice to danger.

A police check could be a deadly trap. Joel needs a document, any document, because in the tide of foreign laborers the police can't be too fussy; he obtains it in the most unexpected manner. Giving an "Aryan" name, he applies for membership at the Berlin Fascist Party branch, where they give courses in Italian to German soldiers and civilians. He attends the lessons, a clandestine Jew in the midst of fellow students who are for the most part SS militiamen, and obtains what he needs: a membership card in the name of Wilhelm Schneider, with his photograph, an enormous fasces, and many stamps. It isn't perfect; an intelligent policeman could uncover the deception with a couple of questions, but once again it's better than nothing. Relying on the tenuous protection of that card, Joel fills the endless days wandering about and meditating a plan of escape.

Luck comes to his aid. By chance he comes into contact with an engineer, an ex-Social Democrat, who gives concreteness to Joel's vague plans. He'll probably be able to get to Vienna, and from there a smuggler will take him into Hungary.

Joel is twenty-one but he looks seventeen, and his features are not Jewish. It seems to him logical to disguise himself in the uniform of the Hitler Youth. Hitler Youth members are not of military age. This means one less checkup, and besides he has always liked to play soldier: his brother Leon, who also lives clandestinely in the city,

goes about wearing a fanciful uniform, and perhaps it's 133
not a bad idea.

The Hitler Youth Joel König/Wilhelm Schneider
leaves for Vienna in May of '43. In his suitcase, among
other things, he has a Bible in Hebrew, a Hungarian
grammar and conversation manual, and an Arab grammar. A knowledgeable traveler, he foresees that in Budapest he will have little time for purchases, and how could
he possibly live in Palestine without being able to speak
with the country's inhabitants in their own language?

In his pocket he still has the yellow star that will
help him to be recognized as a Jew in Vienna. He has
not forgotten to put into the madly suspect suitcase his
two clockwork switches needed to turn on the light and
the hot plate on the Sabbath eve, because a pious Jew is
forbidden to light a fire or its modern equivalents man-
ually; this is servile work that would profane the holy
day. At the baggage inspection, in the crucial moment of
departure from Berlin, Joel distinctly hears the ticking of
one of the devices set off by a jolt: the clerk at the window may hear it and think it is an infernal machine! But
luck once again protects the scatterbrained young man,
and nobody notices a thing.

Here the book unexpectedly ends. The rest of Joel's
adventures are condensed into two short pages of epi-
logue, but they were told to me many years later diffusely,
in great detail, by Joel himself. He told me about his
wandering from one to the other of the last Jews left in
Vienna, by now resigned to their fate. They are terrified
at the sight of the Hitler Youth knocking at their door,

134 and he finds it difficult to prove what he is. They give him money unstintingly: at this point they have no more use for it.

In Vienna Joel is suspected by everyone, and no one is willing to take him in permanently; he goes to the Jewish community center, depopulated by deportations but still functioning through the dedication of a few surviving employees. In the evenings he lets himself be locked in and spends the nights in the latrine, which he locks from the inside. But during the day, like an attentive and curious tourist, he does not neglect to visit the city. When he asks the Viennese the location of the monuments, they answer rudely. Have they noticed that he is Jewish? Or don't they like his uniform? No, they don't like his German. Joel is happy when they mutter behind his back *"Saupreuss"*—"Prussian swine."

The first smuggler betrays and robs him. On the second attempt he gets into Hungary, feels like a free man, and discards the irksome uniform, but in March 1944 he is forced to put it on again because there too the German tanks storm in. Without difficulty, he crosses the border into Rumania, everyone helps him, and he manages to stow away on a Turkish boat that at the height of the war takes him to the Land of the Fathers, at that time a British Mandate. And here, the ultimate paradox, the English Secret Service does not believe his story, which in fact is literally incredible, and at last they throw him into prison under the suspicion of espionage, that blond young man with the German accent who had

crossed all of armed Nazi Europe without the Gestapo's
harming a hair of his head.

But Joel will not write this story. He has graduated
from the university, married, and settled in Holland. He
loves and admires the Dutch, who are tenacious and
lovers of peace, like himself. He is tired, tired of deception and disguises. That is why, in writing as in telling
about his extraordinary adventure, he has not tried to
deceive, to represent himself as different from what he is
and always has been.

Cesare's
Last Adventure

MANY YEARS have passed since I recounted the adventures of Cesare,* and many more since the time, now dark in the distance, when those adventures took place. In some I too had participated, for instance in the purchase-conquest of a hen in the Pripet marshes. In others, Cesare was alone, like the time he took over the task of selling fish for a consortium, but was so moved by the hunger of three children that instead of bartering the fish he gave them away.

Up until now I have not told the most daring of his exploits because Cesare forbade me to do so; having returned to Rome and order, he had built up around himself a family, had a respectable job, a decorous middle-class home, and was loath to recognize himself in the ingenious picaresque hero whom I described in *The Reawakening*. Today, however, Cesare is no longer the in-

---

* *Cesare is a leading character in* The Reawakening, *the sequel to* Survival in Auschwitz.

140 ventive, ragged, and indomitable returnee from the Bye-
lorussia of 1945, or even the irreproachable official of the
Rome of 1965. Incredible as it may seem, he is a pen-
sioner in his sixties, quite serene, quite wise, sorely tried
by fate, and has released me from his injunction, autho-
rizing me to write "before you get bored with it."

So while I am still not bored, I want to tell here of
the way in which Cesare, fed up with the zigzags and
interminable stops of the troop train that was taking us
back to Italy, and impatient to give rein to his inventive
abilities and make use of the monstrous freedom which
fate had bestowed on us after the Auschwitz ordeal,
abandoned us on October 2nd, 1945 because he had decided to return home by plane. If need be after us, but
not like us: not famished, ragged, tired, regimented, es-
corted by the Russians, and on a grueling snail of a train.
He wanted a glorious reappearance, an apotheosis. He
saw the dangers of this, but—"either in a first-class com-
partment, or shoveling coal into the engine."

Our troop train, with its colorful cargo of fourteen
hundred Italians on their tortuous return home, had for
six days been stuck in the rain and mud of a small ham-
let on the border between Rumania and Hungary, and
Cesare was furious with impotence-impatience at the
enforced idleness. He asked me to go with him but I
refused because the adventure frightened me, so he made
some quick arrangements with Signor Tornaghi, said
goodbye to everyone, and left with Tornaghi.

Signor Tornaghi was a *mafioso* from the north, by
profession a fence. He was a sanguine and cordial Mila-

nese, about forty-five. In our previous wanderings he had
stood out due to his almost elegant attire, which for him
was a habit, a symbol of social position, a necessity imposed by his profession. Until a few days earlier he had
flaunted a coat with a fur collar, no less, but then hunger
had forced him to sell it. A partner like this was perfect
for Cesare; he'd never had caste or class prejudices. The
two got on the first train leaving for Bucharest, that is,
in the direction opposite to ours, and during the journey
Cesare taught Signor Tornaghi the main prayers of the
Jewish ritual and got Tornaghi to teach him the Pater,
the Credo and the Ave Maria, because he already had in
mind a minimal program for the first setup in Bucharest.

They got to Bucharest without incident but after
having used up all their meager resources. In the town,
in upheaval due to the war and uncertain about its impending fate, for a couple of days the two engaged in
begging impartially from convents and the Jewish community. As the case required, they claimed to be either
Jews who had survived the slaughter, or Christian pil-
grims fleeing from the Soviets. They didn't collect much,
but they split the proceeds and invested them in clothes:
Tornaghi in order to restore the honest appearance his
profession requires, and Cesare to be ready for the second
phase of his plan. This done, they separated, and of what
happened to Signor Tornaghi nobody ever heard anything.

At first Cesare, wearing a jacket and tie after a
year of shaved skull and the striped garb of a convict,
felt a bit dazed, but it didn't take him long to recover

142 the necessary confidence for the new role he intended to play, which was that of Latin lover, since Rumania (Cesare had quickly found out) was a country much less neo-Latin than the textbooks assert. He didn't speak Rumanian, obviously, or any language other than Italian, but communication difficulties were not an obstacle. On the contrary they came in handy, because it is easier to tell lies when one knows one is not well understood, and besides, in courting techniques articulated language has a secondary function.

After a few unsuccessful attempts, Cesare ran into a girl who met with his requirements: she came from a rich family, and she did not ask too many questions. The information supplied by Cesare about his chosen father-in-law is vague. He was one of the owners of the Ploesti oil wells, and/or a bank director, and he lived in a villa whose gate was flanked by two marble lions. But Cesare is a fish that swims in all waters, and it does not surprise me that he was well received in that family of moneyed bourgeois, who were certainly already frightened by the impending political upheavals in their country. You never know: perhaps a married daughter in Italy could be considered a future bridgehead.

The girl was willing. Cesare was introduced, invited to the villa of the lions; he brought bunches of flowers and became officially engaged. Summoned to an interview with his future father-in-law, he did not hide his situation as a returnee from a Camp. He hinted that for the moment he was short of cash: a small loan, or an advance on the dowry, would come in handy, so that he could set up in some way in the city while waiting for the marriage papers and looking for a job. The girl again proved willing. She was pretty sharp herself and had immediately understood everything—from a victim she had become an accomplice in the swindle. The exotic adventure was to her liking, even if she knew perfectly well it would soon be over, and as for her father's money, she didn't give a damn.

Cesare got the money and disappeared. A few days later, toward the end of October, he boarded an airplane for Bari. So he had won. True enough, he was repatriated *after* us (we had recrossed the Brenner on the 19th of that month), and the swindle had cost him a lot in compromises with his conscience and a love affair cut off halfway, but he was coming back by plane, like a king, as he had promised himself and us when we were mired in Rumanian mud.

That Cesare descended into Bari from the sky there is no doubt. He was seen by numerous witnesses who had rushed to welcome him and they have not forgotten the scene, because as soon as Cesare set foot on the ground he was stopped by the Carabinieri (at that time still Royal Carabinieri). The reason was simple. After the plane had taken off from Bucharest, the employees of the airline had noticed that the dollars Cesare received from the father-in-law, which he had used to pay for the ticket, were counterfeit, and had immediately sent a radio message to the Bari airport. It is not clear whether the ambiguous Rumanian father-in-law had acted in good faith, or got a whiff of the swindle and took pre-

144 ventive revenge, punishing Cesare and at the same time getting rid of him. Cesare was interrogated, sent to Rome with a compulsory travel warrant and a ration of bread and dried figs, interrogated once again, and then released for good.

And this is the story of how Cesare fulfilled his vow; by writing it down I too have fulfilled a vow. It may be imprecise in some details because it is based on two memories (his and mine), and then over long distances human memory is an erratic instrument, especially if it is not reinforced by material mementoes and is instead spiced by the desire (again, his and mine) that the story be a good one. But the detail of the counterfeit dollars is definitely true, and meshes with events that belong to European history in those years. Counterfeit dollars and pounds circulated in abundance toward the end of the Second World War, in all of Europe and especially in the Balkan countries. Among other things, they had been used by the Germans in Turkey to pay the double agent Cicero, whose story has been told many times and in various ways. There too they were a reward for deception.

A proverb says that money is the devil's excrement, and never was money more excremental and more diabolical. It was printed in Germany to inflate monetary circulation in the enemy camp, plant the seed of distrust and suspicion, and for payments of the kind mentioned here. Starting in 1942, most of these banknotes were produced in the Camp of Sachsenhausen, where the SS had collected around a hundred and fifty exceptional prisoners: they were graphic artists, lithographers, photographers, engravers, and counterfeiters who made up the "Kommando Bernhard," a small, top-secret Camp of "specialists" within the confines of the greater Camp, a forerunner of Stalin's *saraski* that Solzhenitsyn would later describe in *The First Circle*.

In March 1945, faced by the advance of Russian troops, the Kommando Bernhard was transferred lock, stock, and barrel, first to Schlier-Redl-Zipf, then (on May 3rd, 1945, a few days before the surrender) to Ebensee, both Camps annexed to Mauthausen. Apparently the counterfeiters worked until the very last day, then the plates were thrown to the bottom of a lake.

Lorenzo's Return

I HAVE ALSO TOLD about Lorenzo elsewhere, but in terms that were deliberately vague. Lorenzo was still alive when I wrote *Survival in Auschwitz*, and the task of transforming a living person into a character ties the hand of the writer. This happens because such a task, even when it is undertaken with the best intentions and deals with a respected and loved person, verges on the violation of privacy and is never painless for the subject. Each of us, knowingly or not, creates an image of himself, but inevitably it is different from that, or, rather, from those (which again are different from one another) that are created by whoever comes into contact with us. Finding oneself portrayed in a book with features that are not those we attribute to ourselves is traumatic, as if the mirror of a sudden returned to us the image of somebody else: an image possibly nobler than ours, but not ours. For this reason, and for other more obvious reasons, it is

150 a good practice not to write biographies of the living, unless the author openly chooses one of two opposed paths: hagiography or the polemical pamphlet, which diverge from reality and are not impartial. What the "true" image of each of us may be in the end is a meaningless question.

Lorenzo has now been dead for many years, and I feel freed from the restraint that previously held me back, and I even feel it my duty to try and recreate the image that I have kept of him in these stories in which are gathered the paralipomena of my first two "Books of Chronicles." I met Lorenzo in June 1944, after a bombing that had torn up the big yard in which both of us were working. Lorenzo was not a prisoner like us; in fact he wasn't a prisoner at all. Officially he was one of the voluntary civilian workers with which Nazi Germany swarmed, but his choice had been anything but voluntary. In 1939 he had been employed as a mason by an Italian firm that operated in France. The war had broken out, all the Italians in France had been interned, but then the Germans had arrived, reconstituted the firm, and transferred it part and parcel to Upper Silesia.

Those workers, even though not militarized, lived like soldiers. They were stationed in a camp not far from ours, slept on cots, had passes on Sundays off, one or two weeks of vacation, were paid in marks, could write and send money to Italy, and from Italy they were allowed to receive clothing and food packages.

The damage done to the buildings in that bombing, one of the first, could be repaired; but bomb fragments and rubble had also hit the delicate machinery that was supposed to start up when the huge complex of the Buna Works was put into production, and here the damage was much greater. The plant management had ordered that the most valuable machines be protected by thick brick walls, and entrusted the construction to Lorenzo's company. My squad at that time was doing transport work in the same area where the Italian masons worked and by pure chance our Kapo picked me to be the helper for two masons I had never seen before.

The two were working on a scaffolding, putting up a wall that was already high. I stayed on the ground and waited for somebody to tell me what to do; the two men were laying bricks at a good pace, without talking, so that at first I did not realize they were Italian. Then one of them, tall, a bit stooped, with gray hair, said to me in execrable German that the mortar was almost gone and that I should bring up the bucket. A full bucket is heavy and cumbersome and held by the handle it bangs against your legs. It must be hoisted up on your shoulder, but that isn't easy. Expert helpers go about it like this: they spread their legs, grab the handle with both hands, lift the bucket, and swing it backward between their legs. Then, using the pendulum thus acquired, they bring the load forward again and in one motion carry it up to the shoulder. I tried, with miserable results: the impetus wasn't strong enough and the bucket fell to the ground, spilling half of the mortar. The tall mason snorted, turned to his companion and said: "Oh well, what do you expect from people like this . . ." then he

152   got ready to climb down from the scaffold. I wasn't dreaming: he had spoken in Italian and with a Piedmontese accent.

We belonged to two different castes of the Nazi universe, and therefore when we spoke to each other we were committing a crime, but we spoke anyway, and as a result we found out that Lorenzo was from Fossano and I was from Turin but had distant relatives in Fossano whom Lorenzo knew by name. I don't think that we said much more to each other, then or later; not because of the prohibition but because Lorenzo almost never spoke. It seemed he didn't need to talk; the little I know about him I've derived only in small part from his scant hints; the greater part is from what I was told by his comrades down there, and later on his relatives in Italy. He wasn't married, he had always been alone; his work, which was in his blood, had invaded him to the point of standing in the way of his human relationships. At the beginning he had worked as a mason in his village and its surroundings, changing employers frequently because he had a difficult personality. If a foreman made a remark about his work, even in the nicest way, he didn't say a word, put on his hat and left. In the winter he often went to work in France on the Côte d'Azur, where there always was plenty of work: he had neither passport nor papers, he left on foot, alone, slept wherever he happened to be, and crossed the border by smugglers' paths. In the spring, he returned the same way.

He didn't speak, but he understood. I don't think I ever asked him for help, because then I didn't have a

clear idea of how these Italians lived and what they could
afford. Lorenzo did everything on his own. Two or three
days after our meeting, he brought me an Alpine troop
mess tin (the aluminum type that holds over two quarts)
full of soup and told me to bring it back empty before
evening. From then on, there always was soup, sometimes
accompanied by a slice of bread. He brought it to me
every day for six months: as long as I was working as his
helper the delivery encountered no difficulty, but after a
couple of weeks he (or I—I can't remember) was transferred to another corner of the workgrounds, and then
the danger increased. The danger was for us to be seen
together: the Gestapo had eyes everywhere and any one
of us seen talking with a "civilian" for reasons not justi-
fied by work risked being tried for espionage. Actually,
the Gestapo had other fears: they feared that the secret
of the Birkenau gas chambers would leak into the outside
world through the civilian workers. Also the civilian
workers ran a risk: whoever among them proved guilty of
illegal contacts with us ended up in our Camp. Not in-
definitely like us; temporarily, for a few months, for the
purpose of *Umschulung*: re-education. I myself made a
point of warning Lorenzo of this danger, but he shrugged
his shoulders without a word.

I shared Lorenzo's soup with my friend Alberto.
Without it we would not have been able to survive until
the evacuation of the Camp. The bottom line is that
that extra quart of soup helped to balance the daily
calorie count. The Camp food supplied us with about
sixteen hundred, which are not enough to live on while

154   working. Lorenzo's soup supplied another four or five hundred calories, still insufficient for a man of medium build, but Alberto and I had already started out small and skinny, and our requirements were lower. It was weird soup. In it we found plum pits, salami peels, once even the wing of a sparrow with all its feathers; another time a scrap of Italian newspaper. I became acquainted with the origin of these ingredients later on when I again saw Lorenzo in Italy: he had told his comrades that among the Jews of Auschwitz were two Italians, and every evening he made the round of his dormitory to collect their leftovers. They too were hungry, even if not as hungry as we, and many managed to do a little private cooking with stuff stolen in the fields or found by scouting around. Later Lorenzo had found a way to take directly from his camp kitchen what was left in the cauldrons, but in order to do so he had to go into the kitchen on the sly, when everyone was asleep at three o'clock in the morning; he did this for four months.

To avoid being seen together, we decided that upon arriving at his place of work in the morning Lorenzo would leave the mess tin in an agreed-upon hiding place under a pile of boards. This arrangement worked for a few weeks, then evidently somebody must have watched and followed me because one day in the hiding place I found neither mess tin nor soup. Alberto and I were humiliated by this affront and also terrified because the mess tin belonged to Lorenzo and his name was scratched on it. The thief could denounce or, more probably, blackmail us. Lorenzo, to whom I immediately reported the theft, said he didn't care about the mess tin, he would get another one, but I knew this wasn't true: it was his army mess tin, he had carried it with him in all his travels, he certainly was attached to it. Alberto didn't stop roaming about the Camp until he identified the thief, who was much stronger than we were and brazenly carried around the beautiful and rare Italian mess tin. My friend hit on a plan: to offer Elias three bread rations, in installments, provided he would agree to recover the mess tin, by fair means or foul, from the hands of the thief, who was a Pole like himself. Elias was the Herculean dwarf I described in *Survival in Auschwitz*, and about whom I have spoken in the story "Our Seal" in this collection. We flattered him, praising his strength, and he accepted. He liked to show off. One morning, before roll call, he confronted the Pole and ordered him to return the stolen mess tin to us. The fellow of course denied everything: he had bought it, not stolen it. Elias attacked him by surprise. They struggled for ten minutes, then the Pole fell into the mud, and Elias, applauded by the audience attracted by the unusual spectacle, triumphantly restored the mess tin to us: from then on he became our friend.

Alberto and I were amazed by Lorenzo. In the violent and degraded environment of Auschwitz, a man helping other men out of pure altruism was incomprehensible, alien, like a savior who's come from heaven. But he was a morose savior, with whom it was difficult to communicate. I offered to have some money sent to his sister, who lived in Italy, in exchange for what he did

156   for us, but he refused to give us her address. However, in order not to humiliate us by this refusal, he accepted from us another form of compensation, more appropriate to the place. His leather workboots were worn out; there was no shoemaker in his camp, and repairs were very expensive in the city of Auschwitz. But in our Camp anyone who had leather shoes could have them repaired free, because (officially) none of us were allowed to have money. So one day he and I exchanged shoes. For four days he walked and worked in my wooden shoes, and I had his repaired by the Monowitz shoemakers, who in the meantime had given me a pair of temporary replacements.

At the end of December, a short time before I fell ill with that scarlet fever which saved my life, Lorenzo had started working near us again and I could again accept the mess tin directly from his hands. I saw him arrive one morning, wrapped in a short, gray-green military cape, surrounded by snow, in the workgrounds devastated by the nighttime bombings. He walked with his long, assured, slow step. He handed me the mess tin, which was bent out of shape and dented, and said that the soup was a bit dirty. I asked him to explain but he shook his head and left, and I did not see him again until a year later in Italy. As a matter of fact, in the soup there were pebbles and grit, and only a year later, almost as an apology, he told me how that morning, while he was on his collection round, his camp had been hit by an air raid. A bomb had fallen close to him and exploded in the soft ground; it had buried the mess tin and burst one of his eardrums, but he had the soup to deliver and had come to work anyway.

Lorenzo knew that the Russians were about to arrive, but he was afraid of them. Perhaps he was right: if he had waited for them, he would have returned to Italy much later, as in fact happened to us. When the front was close, on January 1st 1945, the Germans disbanded the Italian camp, everyone free to go where he pleased. Lorenzo and his comrades had a very vague idea of the geographical position of Auschwitz, and in fact even of its name, which Lorenzo didn't know how to write and pronounced "Suíss," perhaps placing it near Switzerland. Nevertheless he set out on his march, together with Peruch, the colleague who had worked with him on the scaffolding. Peruch was from Friuli, and he was to Lorenzo what Sancho Panza was to Don Quixote. Lorenzo moved with the natural dignity of the person who is oblivious of danger, whereas Peruch, small and sturdy, was restless and nervous, and incessantly turned his head this way and that, with little jerks. Peruch was walleyed; his eyes diverged greatly, almost is if in his permanent anxiety he was striving to look ahead and to both sides at the same time, like a chameleon. He too had brought bread to the Italian prisoners, but secretly and without regularity, because he was too afraid of the incomprehensible and sinister world into which he had been flung. He would hold out the food and immediately hurry off, without even waiting for a thank you.

The two men left on foot. From the Auschwitz station they had taken a railroad map, one of those sche-

158 matic and distorted maps on which only the stations are
indicated, joined by the straight lines of the tracks.
They walked by night, aiming themselves toward the
Brenner, piloting by their map and the stars. They
slept in haylofts and ate potatoes they stole in the fields;
when they were tired of walking they stopped in villages
where there was always some work for two masons. They
rested by working and requested payment in money or
kind. For four months they walked. They arrived at the
Brenner exactly on April 25th, meeting the stream of
German divisions in flight from northern Italy. A tank
opened fire on them with its machine gun but missed
them. After the Brenner, Peruch was almost home and
headed east. Lorenzo continued, still on foot, and in
about twenty days arrived in Turin. He had my family's
address and found my mother, to whom he brought news
of me. He was a man who did not know how to lie; or
perhaps he thought that lying was futile, ridiculous, after
having seen the abomination of Auschwitz and the dis-
solution of Europe. He told my mother I would not return, that the Jews in Auschwitz were all dead, from the
gas chambers, or from work, or killed in the end by the
fleeing Germans (which was almost literally true). Moreover, he had heard from my comrades that at the Camp's
evacuation I was sick. It was best for my mother to resign
herself.

My mother offered him some money so that he
should at least be able to take a train for the last stage of
his journey from Turin to Fossano, but Lorenzo didn't
want it. He had walked for four months and who knows

how many thousands of kilometers; there really was no point in getting on a train. Just past Genola, six kilometers from Fossano, he met his cousin on his cart; the cousin asked him to get on but at this point it would have really been a pity, and Lorenzo arrived home on foot, the way he had always traveled all his life. To him time meant little.

When I too had gotten back, five months later, after my long tour through Russia, I went to Fossano to see him again and bring him a woolen sweater for the winter. I found a tired man; not tired from the walk, mortally tired, a weariness without remedy. We went to the *osteria* for some wine together and from the few words I managed to wrest from him I understood that his margin of love for life had thinned, almost disappeared. He had stopped working as a mason. He went from farm to farm with a small cart buying and selling scrap iron. He wanted no more rules or bosses or schedules. The little he earned he spent at the tavern; he did not drink as a vice but to get away from the world. He had seen the world, he didn't like it, he felt it was going to ruin. To live no longer interested him.

I thought he needed a change of environment and found him a mason's job in Turin, but Lorenzo refused it. By now he lived like a nomad, sleeping wherever he happened to be, even in the open during the harsh winter of '45–'46. He drank but was lucid; he was not a believer, didn't know much about the Gospel, but he then told me something which in Auschwitz I hadn't suspected. Down there he helped not only me. He had other pro-

160 tégés, Italian and not, but he had thought it right not to tell me about it: we are in this world to do good, not to boast about it. In "Suíss" he had been a rich man, at least compared to us, and had been able to help us, but now it was over; he had no more opportunities.

He fell ill, and thanks to some physician friends of mine I was able to get him into a hospital, but they gave him no wine and he ran away. He was assured and coherent in his rejection of life. He was found nearly dead a few days later, and died in the hospital alone. He, who was not a survivor, had died of the survivors' disease.

Story of a Coin

WHEN I RETURNED from Auschwitz, I found in my pocket a strange coin of a lightweight metal alloy, the one you see reproduced here. It is scratched and corroded, and on one face has the Jewish star (the "Shield of David"), the date 1943, and the word *"getto,"* which in German is pronounced "ghetto." On the other face are the inscriptions *"Quittung über 10 Mark"* and *"Der Aelteste der Juden in Litzmannstadt,"* that is, respectively, "Receipt against 10 marks" and "The Elder of the Jews in Litzmannstadt." For many years I didn't pay any attention to it; for some time I carried it in my change purse, perhaps inadvertently attributing to it the value of a good luck charm, then left it in the bottom of a drawer. Recently, information which I gathered from various sources has made it possible for me to reconstruct, at least in part, its history, and it is unusual, fascinating, and sinister.

164   On modern atlases there is no city named Litzmannstadt, but a General Litzmann was and is renowned in
Germany for having in 1914 broken through the Russian
front near Lodz in Poland. In Nazi times, in honor of
this general, Lodz was rechristened Litzmannstadt. During the last months of 1944, the last survivors of the Lodz
ghetto were deported to Auschwitz. I must have found
that coin on the ground at Auschwitz immediately after
the liberation, certainly not before, because nothing I
had on me up till then could have been kept.

In 1939 Lodz had approximately 750,000 inhabitants, and was the most industrialized, most "modern,"
and ugliest of Polish cities. It was a city that, like Man-
chester and Biella, lived on its textile industry, its situation determined by the presence of numerous large and
small mills, mostly antiquated even then, and for the
greater part they had been established several decades
earlier by German and Jewish industrialists. As in all the
cities of a certain importance in occupied Eastern Europe, in Lodz the Nazis were quick to set up a ghetto,
reviving the conditions (harshened by modern ferocity)
of the ghettos of the Middle Ages and the Counter Re-
formation. The Lodz ghetto, already open by February
1940, was the first in order of time and the second in
number of inhabitants after the Warsaw ghetto: it
reached a population of more than 160,000 Jews and
was closed down only in the autumn of 1944. Hence it
was also the most long-lived of Nazi ghettos and this
must be attributed to two reasons: its economic impor-

tance for the Germans, and the disturbing personality of 165
its president.

His name was Chaim Rumkowski, formerly co-owner of a velvet factory in Lodz. He had gone bankrupt and made several trips to England, perhaps to negotiate with his creditors; he had then settled in Russia, where somehow he had again become wealthy; ruined by the revolution in 1917 he had returned to Lodz. By 1940 he was almost sixty, was twice widowed, and had no children. He was known as the director of Jewish charitable institutions, and as an energetic, uneducated, and authoritarian man. The office of president (or elder) of a ghetto was intrinsically dreadful, but it was an office; it represented recognition, a step up on the social ladder, and it conferred authority. Now Rumkowski loved authority. How he managed to obtain the investiture is not known: perhaps thanks to a joke or hoax in the sinister Nazi style (Rumkowski was or appeared to be a fool with a very respectable air; in short, an ideal puppet), perhaps he himself intrigued in order to obtain it, so strong in him must have been the will to power.

It has been proved that the four years of his presidency, or better, his dictatorship, were an amazing tangled megalomaniacal dream of barbaric vitality and real diplomatic and organizational ability. He soon came to see himself in the role of absolute but enlightened monarch, and certainly he was encouraged on this path by his German bosses, who, true enough, played with him but appreciated his talents as a good administrator and man

166 of order. From them he obtained the authorization to mint money, both metal (that coin of mine) and paper—on watermarked paper which was officially issued to him: this was the money used to pay the enfeebled ghetto workers, and they could spend it in the commissaries to buy their food rations, which on the average amounted to 800 calories per day.

Since he had at his disposal a famished army of excellent artists and artisans, anxious at his slightest gesture to jump to do his bidding for a quarter-loaf of bread, Rumkowski had them design and print stamps bearing his portrait, his hair and beard snow-white and gleaming in the light of Hope and Faith. He had a coach drawn by a skeletal nag, and in it rode about his minuscule kingdom, through the streets swarming with beggars and petitioners. He wore a regal cloak, and surrounded himself with a court of flatterers, lackeys, and cutthroats; he had his poet-courtiers compose hymns celebrating his "firm and powerful hand" and the peace and order which thanks to him reigned in the ghetto; he ordered that the children in the nefarious schools, constantly decimated by death from hunger and the Germans' roundups, be assigned essays extolling and praising "our beloved and provident President." Like all autocrats, he hastened to organize an efficient police force, supposedly to maintain order but in fact to protect his person and enforce his control: it was composed of six hundred policemen armed with clubs, and an indefinite number of informers. He delivered many speeches, which in part have come down to us, and whose style is unmistakable. He had

adopted (deliberately? knowingly? or did he uncon-
sciously identify with the man of providence, the "necessary hero," who at that time ruled over Europe?) Mussolini's and Hitler's oratorical technique—that inspired
performance, that pseudo-exchange with the crowd, the
creation of consensus through moral plunder and plaudits.

And yet this personage was more complex than what
appears so far. Rumkowski was not only a renegade and
an accomplice. In some measure, besides making people
believe it, he himself must have become progressively
convinced that he was a *mashiach*, a Messiah, a savior of
his people, whose good he must, at least intermittently,
have desired. Paradoxically, his identification with the
oppressor is flanked by, or perhaps alternates with,
an identification with the oppressed, because man, as
Thomas Mann says, is a confused creature. And he becomes even more confused, we may add, when he is subjected to extreme tensions: he then eludes our judgment,
the way a compass needle goes wild at the magnetic pole.

Although despised, derided, and sometimes beaten
by the Germans, Rumkowski probably thought of himself not as a servant but as a lord. He must have believed
in his authority: when the Gestapo, without advance
notice, seized "his" councillors, he courageously rushed
to their aid, exposing himself to the Nazis' mockery and
blows, which he endured with dignity. Also on other
occasions, he tried to bargain with the Germans, who demanded ever more cloth from his slaves at the looms and
ever-increasing contingents of useless mouths (old people, sick people, children) to send to the gas chambers.

168   The harshness with which he hastened to suppress out-
breaks of insubordination by his subjects (there existed
at Lodz, as in other ghettos, nuclei of obstinate and foolhardy political resistance of Zionist or Communist origin) did not spring so much from servility toward the
Germans as from *lèse majesté*, from indignation at the
offense inflicted on his royal person.

In September 1944, since the Russian front was ap-
proaching the area, the Nazis began the liquidation of
the Lodz ghetto. Tens of thousands of men and women
who until then had been able to withstand hunger, exhausting labor, and illness, were deported to Auschwitz,
anus mundi, ultimate drainage point of the German universe, and almost all of them died there in the gas chambers. In the ghetto about a thousand men were left to
dismantle and take down the precious machinery and
to erase traces of the massacre. They were liberated
shortly after by the Red Army, and to them is owed the
greater part of the information reported here.

About Chaim Rumkowski's final fate there exist
two versions, as though the ambiguity under whose sign
he had lived had extended to envelop his death. According to the first version, during the liquidation of the
ghetto he tried to oppose the deportation of his brother,
from whom he did not want to be separated; a German
officer then proposed that he should leave voluntarily
with this brother, and Rumkowski supposedly accepted.
According to another version, Rumkowski's rescue from
death at the hands of the Germans was attempted by
Hans Biebow, another personage surrounded by a cloud

of duplicity. This shady German industrialist was the 169
official responsible for the ghetto's administration and at
the same time was its contractor. His was an important
and delicate position because the ghetto factories worked
for the German army. Biebow was not a wild animal: he
was not interested in causing suffering or punishing the
Jews for their sin of being Jewish, but in making money
on his contracts. The torment in the ghetto touched him
only indirectly; he wanted the slave-workers to work and
therefore he did not want them to die of hunger; his
moral sense stopped there. Actually *he* was the true boss
of the ghetto and was tied to Rumkowski by a supplier/
purchaser relationship that often leads to a rough
friendship. Biebow, that little jackal, too cynical to take
racial demonology seriously, would have liked to post-
pone the closing down of the ghetto, which for him was
excellent business, and to protect Rumkowski, his friend
and partner, from deportation: which goes to show how
quite often a realist is better than a theoretician. But the
SS theoreticians held a contrary opinion and they were
the stronger. They were *gründlich*, radicals: get rid of the
ghetto and get rid of Rumkowski.

Unable to arrange matters otherwise, Biebow, who
enjoyed good connections, supplied Rumkowski with a
sealed letter addressed to the commander of the Camp
he was being sent to, assured him that it would protect
him, and guaranteed that he would receive special con-
sideration. Apparently Rumkowski requested and got
from Biebow travel arrangements all the way to Auschwitz with the propriety befitting his rank, that is, in a spe-

170 cial coach hooked on to the end of the convoy of freight cars jammed with deportees without privileges; but the fate of Jews in German hands was just one, whether they were cowards or heroes, humble or proud. Neither the letter nor the special coach saved Chaim Rumkowski, the King of the Jews, from the gas of Auschwitz.

A story like this goes beyond itself: it is pregnant, asks more questions than it answers, and leaves us in suspense; it cries out and demands to be interpreted because in it we discern a symbol, as in dreams and signs from heaven, but it is not easy to interpret.

Who is Rumkowski? He's not a monster, but he isn't like other men either; he is like many, like the many frustrated men who taste power and are intoxicated by it. In many of its aspects, power is like drugs: the need for the one and for the other is unknown to those who have not experienced them, but after the initiation, which may be accidental, addiction is born, dependency, and the need for ever larger doses; also born is the rejection of reality and return to infantile dreams of omnipotence. If the hypothesis of a Rumkowski intoxicated with power is valid, it must be admitted that the intoxication arose not because of but despite the ghetto environment, that indeed it is so powerful as to prevail even under conditions that would appear to be likely to extinguish all individual will. In fact, the well-known syndrome of protracted and unchallenged power was only too visible in him: the distorted vision of the world, dogmatic arrogance, convulsive clinging to the levers of command, regarding oneself as above the law.

All this does not exonerate Rumkowski from his re-
sponsibility. That a Rumkowski did exist pains and
rankles; it is likely that, had he survived his tragedy and
the tragedy of the ghetto which he polluted by super-
imposing on it his histrionic figure, no tribunal would
have absolved him, nor certainly can we absolve him on
the moral plane. There are, however, some extenuating
circumstances. An infernal order such as Nazism was
exercises a dreadful power of seduction, which it is difficult to guard against. Instead of sanctifying its victims,
it degrades and corrupts them, makes them similar to
itself, surrounds itself with great and small complicities.
In order to resist, one needs a very solid moral frame-
work, and the one available to Chaim Rumkowski, the
merchant of Lodz, and to all his generation, was fragile.
His is the regrettable and disquieting story of the Kapos,
the smalltime officials in the rear of the army, the func-
tionaries who sign everything, those who shake their
heads in denial but consent, those who say "if I didn't do
this, somebody worse than I would."

It is typical of regimes in which all power rains
down from above and no criticism can rise from below, to
weaken and confound people's capacity for judgment,
to create a vast zone of gray consciences that stands
between the great men of evil and the pure victims. This
is the zone in which Rumkowski must be placed.
Whether higher or lower, it's hard to say; he alone could
clarify it if he could speak before us, even lying, as he
perhaps always lied; he would help us understand him,
as every defendant helps his judge, and helps him even

172 if he doesn't want to, even if he lies, because man's ability to play a role has its limits.

But all of this is not enough to explain the sense of urgency and threat emanating from this story. Perhaps its meaning is different and vaster: we are all mirrored in Rumkowski, his ambiguity is ours, that of hybrids kneaded from clay and spirit; his fever is ours, that of our Western civilization which "descends to hell with trumpets and drums," and his miserable tinsel trappings the distorted image of our symbols of social prestige. His folly is that of the presumptuous and mortal Man as Isabella in *Measure for Measure* describes him, Man who

"Dressed in a little brief authority,
Most ignorant of what he's most assured,
His glassy essence, like an angry ape
Plays such fantastic tricks before high heaven
As makes the angels weep . . ."

Like Rumkowski, we too are so dazzled by power and money as to forget our essential fragility, forget that all of us are in the ghetto, that the ghetto is fenced in, that beyond the fence stand the lords of death, and not far away the train is waiting.

FOR THE BEST IN PAPERBACKS, LOOK FOR THE 🐧

In every corner of the world, on every subject under the sun, Penguin represents quality and variety—the very best in publishing today.

For complete information about books available from Penguin—including Pelicans, Puffins, Peregrines, and Penguin Classics—and how to order them, write to us at the appropriate address below. Please note that for copyright reasons the selection of books varies from country to country.

In the United Kingdom: For a complete list of books available from Penguin in the U.K., please write to *Dept E.P., Penguin Books Ltd, Harmondsworth, Middlesex, UB7 0DA*.

In the United States: For a complete list of books available from Penguin in the U.S., please write to *Dept BA, Penguin*, Box 120, Bergenfield, New Jersey 07621-0120.

In Canada: For a complete list of books available from Penguin in Canada, please write to *Penguin Books Canada Ltd, 10 Alcorn Avenue, Suite 300, Toronto, Ontario, Canada M4V 3B2*.

In Australia: For a complete list of books available from Penguin in Australia, please write to the *Marketing Department, Penguin Books Ltd, P.O. Box 257, Ringwood, Victoria 3134*.

In New Zealand: For a complete list of books available from Penguin in New Zealand, please write to the *Marketing Department, Penguin Books (NZ) Ltd, Private Bag, Takapuna, Auckland 9*.

In India: For a complete list of books available from Penguin, please write to *Penguin Overseas Ltd, 706 Eros Apartments, 56 Nehru Place, New Delhi, 110019*.

In Holland: For a complete list of books available from Penguin in Holland, please write to *Penguin Books Nederland B.V., Postbus 195, NL-1380AD Weesp, Netherlands*.

In Germany: For a complete list of books available from Penguin, please write to *Penguin Books Ltd, Friedrichstrasse 10-12, D-6000 Frankfurt Main I, Federal Republic of Germany*.

In Spain: For a complete list of books available from Penguin in Spain, please write to *Longman, Penguin España, Calle San Nicolas 15, E-28013 Madrid, Spain*.

In Japan: For a complete list of books available from Penguin in Japan, please write to *Longman Penguin Japan Co Ltd, Yamaguchi Building, 2-12-9 Kanda Jimbocho, Chiyoda-Ku, Tokyo 101, Japan*.